THE EXECUTIVE'S GUIDE
TO CREATING AND IMPLEMENTING AN

INTEGRATED MANAGEMENT SYSTEM

OPTIMALLY AND SYNERGISTICALLY
INCORPORATING ISO
AND CORPORATE RESPONSIBILITY
MANAGEMENT STANDARDS
IN RESPONSE TO AN ETHICAL IMPERATIVE

EUGENE A. RAZZETTI

authorHOUSE®

AuthorHouse™
1663 Liberty Drive
Bloomington, IN 47403
www.authorhouse.com
Phone: 1 (800) 839-8640

Published by AuthorHouse 03/03/2016

ISBN: 978-1-5049-8301-3 (sc)
ISBN: 978-1-5049-8299-3 (hc)
ISBN: 978-1-5049-8300-6 (e)

Library of Congress Control Number: 2016903583

Print information available on the last page.

Dedication

This is my fifth book. Like the others, I dedicate it to my wonderful family – living and deceased, the United States Navy, where I learned first-hand about Ethics, Management, Security, and Accountability; and to YOU: the no nonsense professional with a great deal to do and not much time to do it.

G.R.

Foreword

This book covers and revises subjects, texts, and checklists contained in my other four books, but with the goal that each of you creates an <u>Integrated Management System</u> or "IMS". That is, that you optimally implement and employ applicable ISO International Standards without the redundancies and self-serving "busy work" that inevitably comes from separate free-standing Standards. This book also highlights parts of my first book on Ethics and Corporate Responsibility Management. It re-introduces MVO 8000 as an essential pillar in the construction of an Integrated Management System.

I developed this approach for clients while working as an auditor and management consultant in the U.S. and in Central America and as a Military analyst for the Center for Naval Analyses, research of some very fine books, and the 27 years of Military Service that preceded all of it.

The premise of this book and my reason for creating it is simple:

1. Many ISO-certified organizations do not maximize the benefits of their (now) institutionalized focus on Management Review, Internal Auditing, Continual Improvement, and Customer Feedback;

2. *ISO-generated records and reports (although getting better) should either be self-justifying, useful, management tools, or they should be dropped.*

3. *Achieving a "conforming product" is just the beginning. In fact, "conformance with specification" is antithetical to "continuous improvement".*

4. *Profitability is no longer the only metric. Organizations have many other responsibilities – to themselves, employees, stakeholders, regulatory bodies in particular and the community in general.*

5. *Management (regardless of the scenario) contains an "Ethical Imperative". There is no longer justification (or even possibility) of a CEO or a Board NOT knowing of the existence of either a shortcoming or a short cut.*

6. *I want to help all of you to "harden" your organizations against the clear and present danger of cyber-warfare in all its forms.*

I have kept this work as compact as possible, so as to minimize reading time and maximize productivity. I write for no-nonsense CEOs, quality, environmental, and security managers with big responsibilities and limited resources. I refer often to four excellent ISO International Standards. They offer guidance for structuring effective management programs rapidly, regardless of whether or not organizations desire certification by registrars. I invite you to use my approach to Risk Management, as explained an appendix. You will find it an effective and uncomplicated method for developing and monitoring your strategic plans.

Last, I wrote this book not just to show the CEO how to use the ISO Standards synergistically, but also to remind him/her of the need for ethics and ethical behavior at the outset, and without which there is no gain. I believe that everything you need is in this book and my others. However, my books are not the only source for you. It's only important to remember that all you need is in print someplace and there are no excuses for not finding the guidance that you need and implementing it.

Using the checklists provided and taking action on your findings will improve your organization's posture almost immediately.

Good luck, and now let's get to work.

Gene Razzetti

Alexandria, VA

Table of Contents

Introduction

| Sound Management = Success; but |
| Success + Ethics = Greatness |

In recent years, even the most overconfident CEOs have acknowledged the success of structured management systems like ISO 9000, ISO 14000, and some of the others. Security management standards like ISO 27000 (Information Systems Security Management) and ISO 28000 (Supply Chain Security Management) respond to a global imperative that increases every day and can surge at any moment.

In those same recent years, monumental company failures have both underscored the need and created the requirement for CEOs to operate their organizations in accordance with the highest standards of *ethical conduct, moral leadership*, and *responsibility to the community*. CEOs and CFOs are now being required to satisfy themselves and attest in writing regarding the veracity of their organization's documentation. Reliance on outside auditors, to the exclusion of *internal* auditing and controls, inevitably leads to disaster. The ability to conduct effective internal audits is vital for the success of an organization.

I have set up what I call Integrated Management Systems or "IMS" in client organizations, some juggling as many as four ISO Certifications; and both the clients and I have been very pleased with the results.

Points to Remember

✓ An organization, large or small, public or private, should pledge itself to operate not only under the best management practices available, but under the highest standards of moral and ethical conduct as well.

✓ Organizations of any size or mission are vulnerable to cyber or physical attack

✓ An ethical imperative means a command to operate under an exacting set of ethical standards because it is the only morally appropriate action for professional managers to take

✓ The latter half of the twentieth century witnessed the growth of "the right thing to do" in Management[1]

✓ Good companies are no longer defined solely in terms of profit or volume.

✓ Organizations can take a structured approach to Corporate Responsibility Management (CRM), just like the ISO Standards or any other structured best management practices.

1. Combining ISO and CRM requirements

Organizations need to recognize and accept all of the previously unseen responsibilities that involve good citizenship. It is neither easy nor automatic, but for an organization to be a good citizen, it must succeed across a spectrum of challenges that include (in addition to building a profitable business):

- Community responsibility
- Employee health, safety and quality of life
- Environmental compliance.

This book re-introduces MVO 8000, an International Standard which I had the privilege to help create and revise. It is not the intention of this Standard to replace the knowledge and skill of the CEO with a cookbook. Rather, it provides proactive CEOs

---

[1] I capitalize "Management" throughout this book because I hold the term and the professional manager in great respect.

with useful tools to run their organizations as good leaders, managers, and neighbors.

Figure 1 MVO 8000 Corporate Responsibility Management System

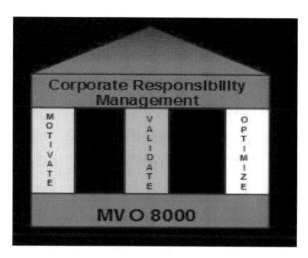

Motivate	Validate	Optimize

MVO 8000 specifies the framework for effective Corporate Responsibility Management. It enables organizations to formulate policies and objectives governing "Corporate Responsibility", incorporating statutory and regulatory requirements, and the requirements of company personnel, stakeholders, suppliers, and the community. The Standard itself does not establish any specific ethical standards or values. MVO 8000 is applicable to every organization planning to:

- Implement, maintain, and improve a Corporate Responsibility Management System
- Comply with the established Corporate Responsibility policies
- Have its Corporate Responsibility Management System certified by an external organization and recognized worldwide

- Confirm by periodic audits that the Corporate Responsibility System is implemented and maintained in accordance with the Standard.

Incorporating MVO 8000 with applicable ISO Standards into an IMS ensures that all processes developed reflect responsibility to the community, as well as technical and security superiority.

Here is the first look at the table that links Corporate Responsibility Management or "CRM" with four of the most well-known ISO Management Standards. Table 1 provides the first look at how ISO Standards and standards of Corporate Responsibility Management can be integrated, for the benefit of everybody. It also shows the inter-relationship of the standards and the many opportunities for synergy.

Table 1 Comparing the ISO Standards with MVO 8000, as part of the IMS

IMS

Requirement/Opportunity	ISO 9000	ISO 14000	ISO 27000	ISO 28000	MVO 8000
Standard and explanation	X	X	X	X	X
Top management involvement	X	X	X	X	X
Employee ownership	X	X	X	X	X
Reflected in Strategic Plan	X	X	X	X	X
Process Oriented	X	X	X	X	X
Resistance at first	X	X	X	X	X
Documentation required	X	X	X	X	X
Training	X	X	X	X	X
Manual and checklists for structure	X	X	X	X	X
Capable of self-audit	X	X	X	X	X
Consolidates other compliance requirements in common OP	X	X	X	X	X
Feedback loops established	X	X	X	X	X
Corrective and Preventive action	X	X	X	X	X
Accountability established	X	X	X	X	X

2. The Ethical Imperative

> *"The only thing necessary for evil to triumph is for good men to do nothing."*
>
> **Edmund Burke**

CEO Note. *Management has an "ethical imperative" to recognize its accountability in any form in which it appears and to exercise that imperative with every resource available.*

All the reference guidance or source material that you need is in print someplace and easy to apply. No more excuses!

Ethics refers to "well-based standards of right and wrong that prescribe what humans do, usually in terms of duties, principles, specific virtues, or benefits to society".[2]

Webster defines an "imperative" as "not to be avoided", "expressing a command", "commanding", "compelling attention or action". You get the idea.

The definitions above, taken together, describe four foundations in which ethics and ethical conduct can be seen:

- Duties: behaviors expected of persons who occupy certain positions
- Virtues: qualities which define what a good person is; moral excellence
- Principles: fundamental truths that form the basis for behavior
- Benefits to society: actions that produce the greatest good for the greatest number.

---

[2] Andre and Velasquez, 1987 "What is Ethics" *Issues in Ethics I, (Fall)*

In <u>The Ethics Primer</u> Professor James H. Svara received the following examples of ethical conduct from his students:[3]

1. Maintain integrity of policies and ordinances (principle)
2. Avoid personal favors (duty)
3. Base actions on public good (duty)
4. Faithfully execute wishes of the elected body (duty)
5. Maintain high standards of morality and honesty (virtue)
6. Avoid conflicts of interests (duty)
7. My lying, stealing, or cheating (principle)
8. Treat everyone fairly (principle)
9. Avoid any actions that advance personal interests (financial) (duty)
10. Full and honest disclosure of public information (duty)
11. Have a strong work ethic (virtue)
12. Maintain objectivity (principle)
13. Provide sound professional advice to elected officials (duty)
14. Avoid even the appearance of impropriety (virtue)
15. Keep everyone informed (duty)
16. Avoid deception and misleading statements (principle)

3. Growth of the "Right Thing to Do"

In 2009, I gave a lecture to Business Administration students at Adelphi University (my alma mater) about what I had seen take place from getting my B.BA from there in 1965 to the present. One slide was entitled "Growth of the Right Thing to do". In my attempt to make history "come alive" to a young and drowsy audience, these are some of the points that the slide covered:

- "Do no harm" became a good place to start when undertaking any venture
- Organizations began to stress product <u>and</u> production safety
- Workers and employees were as important as customers

---

[3] See References

- Establish acceptable safety standards, below which the risks are ethically unacceptable
- Inherently dangerous jobs (e.g., firefighting) were made as safe as possible.
- Employers recognized an ethical obligation (or ethical imperative) to correct an unsafe situation.
- Personnel Management became Human Resource Management
- There was an emerging belief that employees have no reason to engage in immoral or unethical activities for their company
- "Ethics" still wasn't sexy, but was no longer limited to doctors
- Along came inspectors general, ombudsmen, internal auditors
- We shouldn't need whistle blowers, but now we have them
- Organizations want openness and honesty, and develop policies to help employees define their responsibilities regarding ethical breeches by superiors and fellow employees.

Nothing profound here, I was just trying to show the young folks about the exciting world into which they were about to enter – a world for which I believed they were not being prepared. I can't abide with Business Administration "professors" who serve up the same lectures year after year. You can teach Shakespeare for thirty years without changing your lectures, not Business Administration.

4. What makes a "good company"?

Fortune Magazine did a survey to answer the question of what makes a good company in 2009, and this is what it found:

- Long term annual return to stockholders (no surprise there)
- Quality of the products or services (again, you would expect that)

- Quality of the **Management** (how about that!)
- Quality of the **work force** (Yes!); and best of all
- Perceived responsibility to the Community and to the Environment.

Having identified what makes a good company, *Fortune* went on to say that good companies set the standard, not only financially, but with:

- Quality of products and services
- Customer and employee treatment
- Robust and replicable "Codes of Conduct".

Taking the above and applying it to optimally integrating ISO Standards into an organization, we can conclude that organizations wanting to change positively need structured *corporate responsibility management* standards as well as ISO Standards in order to:

- Improve the operating environment as well as the physical environment
- Develop/enhance their character as well as their product
- Make ethical conduct a way of life
- Become the best possible neighbors
- Bullet-proof customer relationships
- Effectively self-audit and not rely on outside regulations or regulators.

Now you know what this book is about. Good luck and let's get to work.

5. Organization of this book

Section One of this book: *Preparing for the IMS*, provides the CEO and the staff with the building materials and mindsets they need to create, implement, and (believe it or not) prosper from the use of an Integrated Management System or "IMS". It goes on to describe what the structure will look like. The ultimate form your IMS will take should both vary with and scrupulously reflect the mission of your organization and your management style.

Section Two, *Building the Integrated Management System,* takes you through ISO Standards 9000 (Quality Management Systems), ISO 14000 (Environmental Management Systems), ISO 27000 (Information Systems Security Management), and ISO 28000 (Supply Chain Security Management). It then re-introduces MVO 8000 (Corporate Responsibility Management).

Most readers will be familiar with the first two ISO Standards, but likely not the latter. I highly recommend that, whatever else you do, you familiarize yourselves with them and realize that, in these times, organizations are incredibly threatened and vulnerable – more so than ever before in my (long) lifetime.

The checklists and appendices will help you to both build expeditiously and monitor effectively the progress of your IMS.

Again, good luck, and now let's get to work.

Section One

Preparing for the IMS

Chapter One: What is an Integrated Management System?

CEO Note: Creating and implementing an integrated management system is, in my opinion, the ultimate management consulting engagement and the best thing a management consultant can do for an organization.

Points to Remember

✓ The major ISO Standards are alike in many ways and impose the same requirements – many of which can be combined. Risk Management is a perfect example, followed by Internal Auditing, Documentation, and Management Review.

✓ When the ISO Standards are combined synergistically (i.e., integrated), the "value add" makes the Standards greater than if they were all independent of each other.

✓ Audits, like the inspections of old, can be nothing more than "snapshots" of a condition. The picture you get today may suggest something about yesterday, but nothing definite about tomorrow.

✓ If Management (not to mention the ISO Registrar) expects its people to <u>conform</u> simultaneously to the requirements of several Standards, it is not unreasonable that they be operating together; and that "simultaneous" audits and reviews be part of the strategy.

This book explains the concept, the strategy, and the implementation process for an effective integrated management system or "IMS".

Overview

Many members of the ISO family of International Standards are *measurably effective* when used individually, *predictably valuable* when used together, but *synergistically dynamic* when **integrated**.

An organization that is certified to three of the ISO International Standards (let's say ISO 9000, ISO 14000, and ISO 28000), if it complies with the letter of the Standards, faces three sets of:

- Internal audits and audit schedules
- Threat analyses
- Risk Management strategies and associated justifications
- Management reviews
- Documents and records
- Manuals and/or operating procedures.

That burdensome approach may prove *conformity*, but it may not prove *control*, and certainly does not prove *management*.

In fact, it suggests an absence of management. It wastes fiscal and human capital and contributes to a tokenistic, perfunctory, implementation; until (like the Holy Roman Empire) the system eventually crushes under its own weight.

The seminal enhancement of ISO 9001:2000 over the 1994 version was that it took the focus from discreet functions (e.g. warehousing or assembly) to holistic *processes*, wherein all the organization's discrete functions are conducted as part of an overall process, and with due regard for their impact on each other. Simultaneous auditing of those mutually supporting functions to more than one ISO Standard is, accordingly, logical

4

and appropriate. Moreover, it supplements the value of the internal audit, which is a "value add" function already, or it isn't worth the doing.

A Mindset is a terrible thing to waste

1. Process Approach and Mindset

A simple explanation of an Integrated Management System (IMS) would be that it is a logical uniting of multiple (otherwise stand-alone) ISO Standards. It is, however, more than that. To maximize their value, multiple ISO Standards should be merged *synergistically*; that is, combined so that the value of the (complete) IMS is greater than the sum of the individual Standards.

We define "synergy" and get into its *technical* aspects elsewhere. First, however, we need to examine the *programmatic* aspects. Creating an IMS requires not just being organized, and replicable to the point of certification, it requires a synergistic *mindset* that says:

- This is worth doing – thoroughly and sustainably
- The manuals, operating procedures, and/or flowcharts (i.e., what you want your people to do) must reflect the letter, spirit, and best practices of the Standards – that's what makes them credible
- There must be added value, as the established processes will be better than they would be had the requirements of the Standards been implemented separately.

With that in mind, the synergistic merging of the Standards into an IMS is a function of the mission and operations of the specific organization and the Standards selected, and every actual IMS implementation will be different.

Table 1-1 compares ISO 9000 (Quality), ISO 14000 (Environmental), ISO 27000 (Information Systems Security) and ISO 28000 (Supply Chain Security) Management Systems, plus the Corporate Responsibility Management Standard MVO 8000. You can see again how alike they are in their prerequisites. It follows that their strategies and approaches will also be alike.

Table 1- 1 Common ISO Standard Characteristics

IMS

Requirement/Opportunity	ISO 9000	ISO 14000	ISO 27000	ISO 28000	MVO 8000
Standard and explanation	X	X	X	X	X
Top management involvement	X	X	X	X	X
Employee ownership	X	X	X	X	X
Reflected in Strategic Plan	X	X	X	X	X
Process Oriented	X	X	X	X	X
Resistance at first	X	X	X	X	X
Documentation required	X	X	X	X	X
Training	X	X	X	X	X
Manual and checklists for structure	X	X	X	X	X
Capable of self-audit	X	X	X	X	X
Consolidates other compliance requirements in common OP	X	X	X	X	X
Feedback loops established	X	X	X	X	X
Corrective and Preventive action	X	X	X	X	X
Accountability established	X	X	X	X	X

2. The continuing role of Risk Management

The major ISO Standards contain an implicit or an explicit requirement for the organization seeking certification to have an effective risk management program; one that (among other things):

- Identifies threats, criticalities, and vulnerabilities to the organization and its missions
- Assigns consistent (albeit subjective) values to reflect established metrics and measures of effectiveness
- Feeds the findings into the strategic planning and decision making processes.

The terms *risk analysis, risk assessment,* and *risk management,* often used interchangeably, can mean a variety of different concepts and/or metrics. In point of fact, there is no one single approach to Risk Management. The challenge to risk analysts is to frame the output of the analysis in a manner that makes sense to the decision makers and that clearly and concisely represents the present and predicts the future. Approaches and strategies can be as simple or complex as the processes they were made to assess. However, simpler is almost always better, and using a spreadsheet that automatically computes and displays the assessments is better still.

The objective is the continual improvement through continual identification and reduction of risk, as suggested in figure 1-1.

Figure 1- 1 Continual Risk Assessment and Minimization

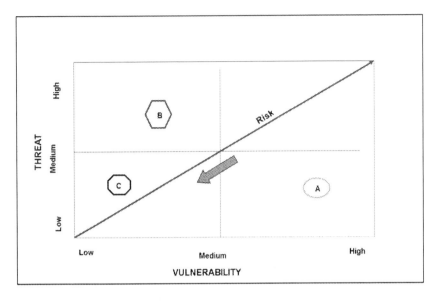

With a comprehensive risk management program as part of your IMS, and by complying with all the applicable ISO Standards:

- Risks are identified, as well as their effects and interactions
- Contingency plans/courses of action can be developed, including preemptive responses which mitigate or reduce the potential impacts
- Expected costs can be reduced, and an appropriate balance between costs and risk exposure achieved, usually with a reduced risk exposure
- Feedback into the design phases and planning stages is developed as part of the evaluation of "risk vs. expected cost" balance
- Opportunities and responses are recognized and gamed in advance
- The integration of planning and cost control is improved
- Members of project teams develop an analytical understanding of the likely problems and responses in

their own areas, and problems in other areas which will impact on them

- Specific problem areas receive focus, and further analysis is pursued
- Management is provided with a means of signaling trends and aligning organization-wide goals and objectives.
- Knowledge and judgments are formalized and documented, making subsequent projects easier to manage, even if the original team members are not available, plus management can create the ability to push back opinions of other decision makers
- External technical, environmental, and political influences are specifically measured in direct relation to internal issues, and appropriate strategies are developed reflecting both
- Probability distributions can be developed for estimating costs and completion dates.

Figure 1-2 depicts a notional outcome of the risk management process. More on this later.[4]

Figure 1- 2 Displaying risk management findings and strategies

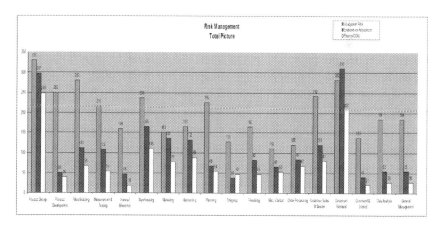

---

[4] I describe this process in my book: *Fixes That Last – The Executive's Guide to Fix It or Lose It Management* and later in this book.

9

3. The continuing quest for Synergy

Redundancy ➡ Commonality ➡ Synergy

Synergy + Metrics ➡ Objectives

Webster defines "*synergy*" as the combined or cooperative action of two or more stimuli for an enhanced effect. It means that the whole becomes *greater* than the sum of its parts, and that 1 + 1 can equal 2.5[5].

In the development of an integrated management system, and all the potentially beneficial synergies, Management must first look for three progressively supporting activities:

- **Redundancy**: wherein several organizations perform *similar* activities to achieve the same objectives; leading to
- **Commonality**: wherein several organizations perform *the same* activities to achieve the same objectives; leading to
- **Synergy**: wherein one organization, by doing *one activity for several similar organizations*, achieves more than could be accomplished by all the similar organizations each doing the same activity.

In business, synergy can mean that when separate departments within an organization cooperate and interact, they become more productive and efficient than if they had operated separately. For example, it is more efficient for each department in a small organization to deal with one (centralized) marketing department, rather than each creating a marketing function of its own.

An absolute requirement for the creation and use of synergies, especially for an integrated management system, is a *mindset*.

---

[5] This section is from an article I wrote for the "Defense Acquisition Management Journal" entitled: "*Synergy, Innovation You Can Measure*".

That is, an instinctive response from Management that says one plus one must equal 2.5 or it's not worth the doing.

Management can work more effectively with "synergy" than with "innovation" because synergy can be quantified, whereas innovation (if not the result of pursuing synergy) often cannot.

Implementing synergies in an integrated management system begins with aligning them and their associated metrics with the gaps or shortcomings to be addressed in the development of organizational objectives.

4. Simultaneous vs. sterile audits

Like the inspections of old, audits are sometimes nothing more than "snapshots" of a condition. The picture you get today suggests something about yesterday, but little about tomorrow. Discreet audits of discreet functions can become sterile. Their findings are of limited interest because the impact of those findings on the total organization is not assessed. An integrated management system audit, on the other hand, takes a holistic picture of a function or process, measuring simultaneously the impact of a discovered nonconformity on:

- The quality of the product or service
- Workplace safety
- The generation of (sometimes hazardous) waste and/or the impact on the community and the environment
- The state of training, qualification, and work ethic
- The security of proprietary or customer information
- The impact of the organization on the community.

In this same holistic approach, integrated management system audits tend be not only more meaningful in their *conduct*, but also in their *outcome*. Specifically:

- Structured, replicable, and continuous feedback loops are established for continuous improvement. These, in

11

turn, can support the absence of stigmas – if something's wrong, you fix it. Moreover, feedback (positive or negative) becomes an obligation (no more: "no news is good news")

- Customer involvement enhances, of necessity
- Responsibilities are assigned for immediate corrective or preventive action.
- Fixing a nonconformity in one Standard automatically fixes it in the others
- Only one management manual (operational, not administrative)
- Up-to-date goals and objectives, reassessed periodically as situations change
- Standard operating procedures (revised as necessary)
- Documentation and records become management tools, not recurring reports.

Audit quality should replace audit quantity

Several years ago, I conducted an audit of ISO 9000, 14000, and 28000 in one of the two major ports in Guatemala. I discovered that all three Standards could be audited simultaneously, as long as I had sufficiently prepared and had a comprehensive (but manageable) checklist. There was simply no point in scheduling and conducting three separate audits of the same facility (or process), when a single hike through the facilities would do.

The Port Authority liked the concept. They also liked the attendant amalgamation of the three manuals and sets of operating procedures and flowcharts, not to mention the fact that only one Management Representative was required.

The auditees liked it better, too, because audit quality replaced audit quantity. Also, if Management expects its people to *conform* simultaneously to the requirements of several Standards, it is reasonable and appropriate to schedule "simultaneous" audits.

Referring back to table 1-1, you can see how alike these Standards are in structure, requirements, and expectations. You can also see how difficult it would be to manage all three Standards separately.

5. Best of all, only one comprehensive Management Review

ISO 9000 states that: *"Top management shall review the organization's quality management system, at planned intervals, to ensure its continuing suitability, adequacy, and effectiveness."* The stated requirements of other major ISO Standards are similar. Accordingly, it is not difficult to develop a management review process that satisfies the requirements of all the Standards in the Integrated Management System. There is need for only one (integrated) Management Review, covering all the ISO requirements in a holistic and mutually supporting approach.

As a result:

- Feedback, follow-up, and accountability (absolute requirements in any organization) are well-structured and robust;
- Documents and reports are streamlined and standardized;
- Risks are identified and assessed;
- Budgets are prioritized and defensible; and
- Training and qualification programs become more focused and fruitful.

6. Building the Integrated Management System

"Always bear in mind that your own resolution to success is more important than any other thing" **Abraham Lincoln**

Table 1-2 IMS Development checklist

Statement	Quality	Env.	Info. Sec.	SC Sec	CRM	Remarks
Gather ISO Standards	X	X	X	X	X	
Review/Update Strategic Plan	X	X	X	X	X	Goals and Objectives
Develop SWOT	X	X	X	X	X	All sites
Conduct Threat Analysis	X	X	X	X	X	All sites
Establish Metrics and MOE	X	X	X	X	X	All sites
Conduct Gap Analyses	X	X	X	X	X	All sites
Complete customer survey	X	X	X	X	X	All sites
Conduct Risk Analysis/ Develop Risk Mgmt. strategy	X	X	X	X	X	All sites
Review Documentation (i.e., flow charts, BMPs, Customer requirements Code of Ethics)	X	X	X	X	X	All sites
Structure/Revise Internal Audits; Develop Audit Schedule	X	X	X	X	X	All sites
Develop Steering Committee and Management Representative	X	X	X	X	X	Establish Mindsets (Note 1)
Develop Management Review process	X	X	X	X	X	Establish basic agenda

Develop/Revise documentation Manual, OPs and/ or flow charts	X	X	X	X	X	All sites
Develop/revise training and qualification standards/ Conduct training	X	X	X	X	X	All sites
Establish Feedback, Follow-up, and Accountability lines and loops	X	X	X	X	X	Internal and external

Note 1, Mindsets: Verification and Validation, Continuous Improvement, Value-Add, Conformity isn't Enough, Best Management Practices, Management Tools vs. Recurring Reports, and Situational Awareness

Figure 1-3 summarizes all the different inputs to an effective IMS.

Figure 1-3 IMS input fishbone diagram

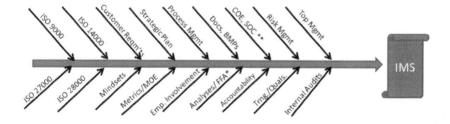

ISO 9001:2015 removes the requirement for a manual, providing more discretion to Management. This is welcomed, but not surprising, because over the years, the "Manual" has become a simple restatement of the Standard. Depending on the process to be documented, an Operating Procedure (OP) and/or a process flow chart will do as well.

An ISO 9000 – compliant OP can achieve compliance with other applicable ISO Standards by adding the appropriate requirements to it. The completed product is an "IMS OP", tailored for the specific organization, as described in figure 3-2. Note the common (and indispensable) management essentials: Risk Management, Internal Auditing, and Management Review.

Figure 1-4 describes how to structure an operating procedure (OP) consistent with the requirements (and benefits) of an integrated management system.

Figure 1-4 An operating procedure (OP) for the IMS

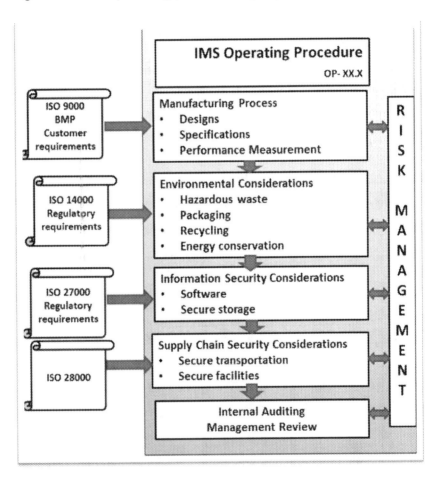

Summary

Putting it all together in a value proposition:

- ✓ You have sponsorship at the top, holistic (but tailored) strategic planning, and better relationships across departments
- ✓ All the Standards are similar, mutually supportive, and gather strength from each other
- ✓ Fixing a nonconformity in one Standard fixes it in the others
- ✓ You have only one (dynamic) Management Manual (likely with two volumes)
  - ○ Operational, not administrative
  - ○ Up-to-date goals and objectives
  - ○ Standard operating procedures (revised as necessary)
  - ○ Documentation and records (management tools, not recurring reports)
  - ○ One Management Representative[6]

- ✓ One area (e.g., Management Review)can be audited for all Standards simultaneously
- ✓ One Management Review covering the requirements of all the applicable Standards.
- ✓ Last but not least: continuous, sustainable, quantifiable improvement in all Standards.

---

[6] ISO 9001:2015 eliminates the requirement for a designated Management Representative. However, the term and the position may be around for the next few years.

Chapter Two: IMS Building Blocks

The Introduction described the importance of merging standards of performance with standards of corporate responsibility. Chapter One provided an overview of an Integrated Management System or "IMS". This chapter provides some necessary building blocks for a successful IMS.

Points to Remember

✓ The first thing that an organization needs is a strategic plan, dynamic and capable of implementation, measurement, review, and revision.
✓ Internally audit your organization; don't rely on outsiders.
✓ Establish measures of effectiveness.
✓ Benchmark your operations against established standards and best management practices.

1. The Strategic Plan – You Need One of These

There have been many excellent books written on the subject of strategic planning, and just as many that are trendy rather than excellent, and many consultants have been made rich covering somebody else's conference room walls with butcher paper and ink from magic markers. It is my purpose to repeat or contradict any of them. Neither is it to recommend your optimal approach to strategic planning (e.g., planning officers/staffs, teams, top down – bottom up, blah-blah). You decide the best approach; just ensure that:

- You have a vision of how you want your organization to look to the outside world in general and your stakeholders in particular.
- You have a clearly defined mission for your organization
- You have identified your gaps.

Then, after identifying your gaps, ensure that you develop:

- Goals for your organization covering all pertinent areas of the mission and all areas in which gaps have been identified.
- Objectives, in which each of the identified goals is quantified in accordance with established metrics.[7]
- A Plan of Action and Milestones (POA&M) from the objectives, assigning personnel/divisions by name and tracking progress.[8]

It goes without saying (so why am I saying it?) that all of this requires buy-in from your stakeholders. The Strategic Plan must belong to them as well as to you.

---

[7] A goal might be to reduce widget defects; an objective is to reduce widget defects by 10% each quarter.

[8] A POA&M for the above would be the Assembly Department Manager will cause a 10% defect reduction and report the status 30 June. Many organizations start with management-directed goals and never translate them into accepted and quantified objectives and milestones.

Figure 2-1 Starting with a Vision for the Organization and drilling down to actionable Milestones.

2. An effective program of internal auditing – see the next chapter

3. Metrics and Measures of Effectiveness

It has been said that what can't be measured can't be managed. CEOs must have the ability to subjectively and objectively quantify the success or failure of their operations, products, or services. They must be able to measure the components of those operations and compare their findings with established standards. With the right mindset and the right metrics, CEOs and managers can:

- Optimally plan an entire throughput process, based on missions, load locations, and available resources
- Establish completion goals (pieces/day, number of days required, required deadlines)
- Evaluate operations in progress, and assess the ability of assigned resources to meet the established goals.

Once the optimal metrics and measures of effectiveness have been identified, CEOs and managers can employ them to assess all areas of operations, meaningfully quantifying:

- Decision making processes
- Intelligence collection
- Risk, vulnerability, and the allocation of limited resources
- Optimal reporting procedures
- Plotting and prediction procedures
- Alternative courses of action.

4. Feedback, Follow-up, and Accountability – See each in the Glossary

5. Due Diligence

Due diligence can be summarily defined as "investigation by or on behalf of an intended buyer of a business to check that it has the desired assets, turnover, profits, market share positions, technology, customer franchise, patents and brand rights, contracts and other attributes required by the buyer or claimed by the seller."[9]

That means, essentially, to make sure that all the facts regarding an organization are available and have been independently verified (in a merger or acquisition, for example). Designated due diligence personnel (e.g., a team of financial, technical, and/ or legal experts) review and analyze all operative documents and interview key organization personnel.

6. Management Commitment

Top management commits to the mission of the organization, involves itself in all aspects, and reviews the organization's management systems at planned intervals, to ensure continuing suitability, adequacy, and effectiveness. Management Reviews include assessing opportunities for improvement and the need

---

[9] Crainer, S (Ed), *Handbook of Management – The State of the Art,*

for changes to the IMS, including policy and objectives, threats, and risks.

Easier said than done? You bet! However, Management Commitment is what's needed in the credible practice of Management.

7. Benchmarking and Gap Analysis

Benchmarking has aptly been described as "seeking out, identifying, and attempting to emulate and improve on best practices where found". You need to see where you are relative to where you should be, as demonstrated in the gap analysis diagram below.

Figure 2.2 Benchmarking and Gap Analysis

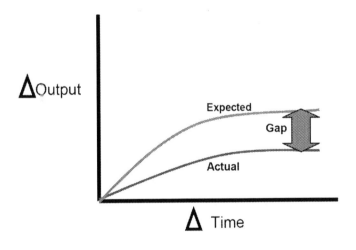

Internal benchmarking examines your own activities taking place inside your walls. Areas always ready (and in need of) internal benchmarking include, but are not limited to:

- Facilities
- Manufacturing and material handling processes
- Administration
- Training
- Costs of doing business

- Inventory levels and stock turnover
- Waste, work in progress, reject rates
- Other work sites in the same company (as applicable)
- Purchasing/procurement
- Contracting practices.

External benchmarking areas include, among others:

- Customer satisfaction (on-time delivery, reliability/defect reports, etc.)
- Competitors' products
- Recommendations from external consultants and auditors
- Public databases, tradeshows, seminars, and workshops
- Annual reports of other companies
- Government agencies
- ISO 9000, ISO 14000, and other international standards

8. Cost-Benefit Analysis

Cost is the amount of resources (e.g., funding) needed to achieve a particular objective. *Cost analysis* therefore can be defined as estimation (in monetary terms) of the amount of resources that have been or will have to be expended to accomplish some objective. The primary purpose of cost analysis is to provide management with data with which to make a correct decision. Cost-benefit analysis takes those required resources identified and predicts:

- At what point (if at all) benefit is realized from amounts expended (the cross-over point)
- The period or range during which benefits justify costs (favorable cost/benefit position)
- The point at which costs exceed benefits (where the two meet again).

The purpose of cost–benefit analysis is to provide management with quantitative data for informed decision making. When assessing multiple approaches, managers must evaluate the costs and benefits of alternatives, in order to determine the optimum decision and strategy. That is, the cost-benefit relationship that best satisfies the organization's requirement. Managers need to ensure that the analyses reflect incremental costs, depreciation, scrap value, environmental disposal fees, and the like. Anything less than a "cradle to grave" analysis invalidates the data by misstating costs and (naturally) the points at which benefit begins and ends.

Figure 2-3 describes the relationship of cost and benefit over to time. This is shown in its most basic form. Managers can modify it to suit their specific requirements. You need to note that at some point cost will exceed value, and it then becomes time to provide a different or modified product or service.

Figure 2.3 Cost-Benefit Analysis

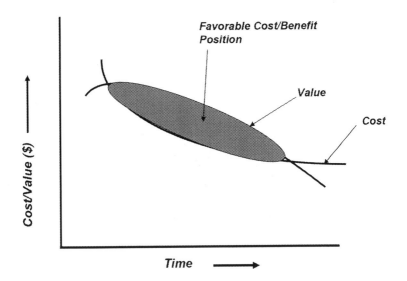

9. Mindsets

Throughout this book, I discuss mindsets, by which I mean fixed mental attitudes or dispositions that predetermine a person's interpretations and responses to situations.

CEOs and managers should think about and establish mindsets along the following lines:

- Verification and Validation (see glossary)
- Continuous Improvement
- Value-Add
- Conformity isn't enough
- Best Management Practices
- Management Tools vs. Recurring Reports
- Synergies

Figure 2-4 is the famous diagram describing continuous (or continual) improvement. It has been used in the ISO Standards for many years, and presupposes a mindset of continual improvement.

Figure 2-4 Continuous Improvement

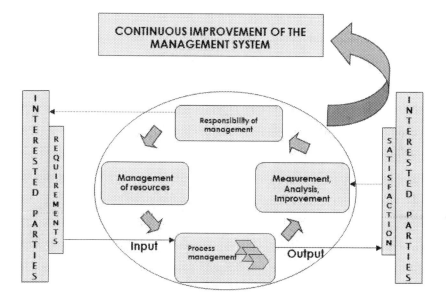

Summary

This chapter discussed the effective building blocks for an effective IMS. There is nothing new or revolutionary. Management commitment is essential; nothing works without that, at least not for long.

Management commitment manifests itself on a continuous basis through the internal auditing process, which is the subject of the next chapter.

Section Two

Constructing the Integrated Management System

Chapter Three: Internal Auditing – the heart of the IMS

✓ Developing an internal auditing capability within a client organization can be as important to the continued success of that organization as the consulting engagement itself.

✓ An "audit" is a systematic, independent, and documented process for obtaining audit evidence and evaluating it objectively to determine the extent to which audit criteria are fulfilled. "Internal audits" are audits conducted by on behalf of the organization (client) itself for internal purposes, and can form the basis of the organizations self-declaration of conformity (compliance).

✓ A well planned, effective, internal auditing program should consider the relative importance of the processes and areas to be audited.

✓ The success of an organization is the sum of the effectiveness of management authority, responsibility, and accountability. They are, in turn, the sum of the manner in which management deals with the findings of the internal audits.

Management consultants like me routinely help to set up or reorganize companies in order to help them to reach their full potential. However, with a little more effort, we can give them an *ongoing* capability to assess and improve themselves on a continuing basis. Management consultants who can audit processes and train organizations to audit themselves, can be heroes to their clients, as well as permanent "value-adds". Audits provide practical, impartial, feedback, and can save large amounts of time and money.

Structured, proven, management programs such as ISO 9000 and ISO 14000, underscore the value of effective *internal* auditing of organization processes toward a goal of continual improvement. An organization must be able to identify and correct its own shortcomings, without relying on outsiders. Again, developing an internal auditing capability within a client organization can be as important to the continued success of that organization as the consulting engagement itself.

Years ago, one of my many and often-frustrated mentors[10] had a sign in his office that read: "*Expect What You Inspect*". That meant, as he "patiently" explained: If you check on something routinely, before long you will be happy with what you see. If you hardly ever check it, you'll likely be unhappy when finally *forced* not only to see it, but also to fix it, and if you inspect frequently, the area or function eventually operates well and continues to improve.

Outside auditors audit against known standards and look for trends and identify corrective actions; internal auditors should do the same.

Looking critically at internal operations and processes and comparing them with approved standards is the basis of internal auditing. An organization can develop its own internal auditing capability, or (you guessed it) it can hire a management consultant. Either way, an effective program of internal auditing can provide a comprehensive, self-sustaining, evaluation and improvement capability for an organization. Its structure and

---

[10] Often frustrated by me, I'm afraid.

administration can be simple, but its contribution can be vital to the client, as well as lucrative (and satisfying) to the consultant.

Organizations don't always do all the work required to establish effective internal auditing programs or adequately qualify internal auditors. As a result, audits tend to be perfunctory, biased, or sporadic. More important, critical audit findings may not be declared, or corrective actions instituted). Instead of executing a meaningful measure of organizational effectiveness, unqualified and unmotivated auditors only waste time, annoy busy people, and turn everyone off to the potential benefits of internal auditing.

1. Auditing to "Approved Standards"

"Quality," in its most simplistic definition, means conformance with standards. Approved process standards are vital to the continuous improvement and competitiveness of an organization. They form the criteria with which meaningful self-assessment can be made. The ever-changing global marketplace has placed great emphasis on the importance of quality in all goods and services.[11]

2. Internal Auditing

The best way to describe internal auditing is with two definitions from the ISO 9000 Standard.[12]

- An "audit" is a systematic, independent, and documented process for obtaining audit evidence and evaluating it

---

[11] The Malcolm Baldridge National Quality Improvement Act of 1987 (Pub L 100-107), signed by President Reagan, established the Malcolm Baldridge National Quality Award, named in honor of the Secretary of Commerce. This award is presented to organizations who have achieved excellence in their endeavors, as assessed by established and exacting evaluation standards and criteria.

[12] American Society for Quality, ANSI/ISO/ASQ Q 9001 – 2015 Standard, Quality Press, Milwaukee, WI, 2008

objectively to determine the extent to which audit criteria are fulfilled.

- "Internal audits" are audits conducted by on behalf of the organization (client) itself for internal purposes, and can form the basis of the organizations self-declaration of conformity (compliance).

Properly planned and well-implemented internal audits provide management with an ongoing, credible, and structured measure of how well the organization is achieving its goals and objectives.

> **CEO Note:** *Remember: Management can identify its own problems, or it can hear about them from stakeholders.*

What does an Internal Audit look like?

Here are some characteristics of an effective internal audit program. I'll start with the obligatory acronym - that way we'll get it over with:

"SMART": *Scheduled – Measurable – Accurate – Repeatable – Timely.*

There, that wasn't so bad.

The first step is to define and **schedule** every "audit-able" process for an audit at least once per year. "Surprise" audits are marginally effective, upset auditees, and reinforce a "pass-fail" mindset. Processes compared against approved standards (pounds of waste produced, finished products per hour, etc.) are **measurable**. Checklists are important for audit structure and repeatability[13]. Audit findings are therefore **accurate.** Findings generated during the audit must be **repeatable**. That is, a different auditor, auditing to the same standard, should come up with the same findings.

---

[13] Please see the checklists in the Appendix.

Last, the audit should be **timely.** Discovering a problem that occurred six months ago, or has been occurring regularly for the last six months is not as good as finding it early. As a manager, you already knew that. Sorry!

Internal auditors should be independent of the processes being audited, and should never audit their own work. Some of an auditor's (or a consultant's) most challenging moments can be trying to assure middle managers that their jobs will not be jeopardized or forfeit as a result of audit findings. To do this with genuine credibility requires real, continuing, and committed support from Top Management. A commitment to continual improvement cannot exist in an atmosphere of retribution or retaliation. It just drives the troops deeper into the foxholes.

The internal auditing program must be organization-specific, to ensure compatibility with the other management systems in the organization. A "cookie-cutter" or plagiarized system will achieve only limited success at best. For this reason, international quality standards, like the ISO Standards, provide only "guidelines," and leave the client organization to fill in specifics. Additionally, a well-planned, effective, internal auditing program should consider the relative importance of the processes and areas to be audited. That is, *first things first.*

The first thing an experienced auditor does is to review the last audit. Specifically:

- When was the last audit;
- What were the findings,
- Were preventive or corrective actions developed and implemented, and
- Were the preventive or corrective actions effective?

This says a great deal about how seriously the organization takes its internal audit function.

What benefits can Internal Auditing bring to the organization? Summarized below are key areas of management that can be improved by an effective internal auditing program. Look through these, and as you do, please think of how they apply to your organization.

3. Auditing Continual Improvement

The ISO 9000 International Quality Management Standard requires Management to use the findings from internal audits to develop and implement improvements to the existing processes on a continuous basis. The premise is that every process can be improved, and that no process is ever "finished" or "completed." Auditing of processes (depending on the capability of the auditor) will nearly always result in the identification of deficiencies and recommendations for improvement. Management can constantly improve its operations, or it can hear about shortcomings from the customers.

Figure 3-1 describes the role of internal auditing in continual improvement. Feedback is vital; the greatest internal audit discoveries may be lost if not reported through a timely and effective feedback loop.

Figure 3-1 Auditing continual improvement

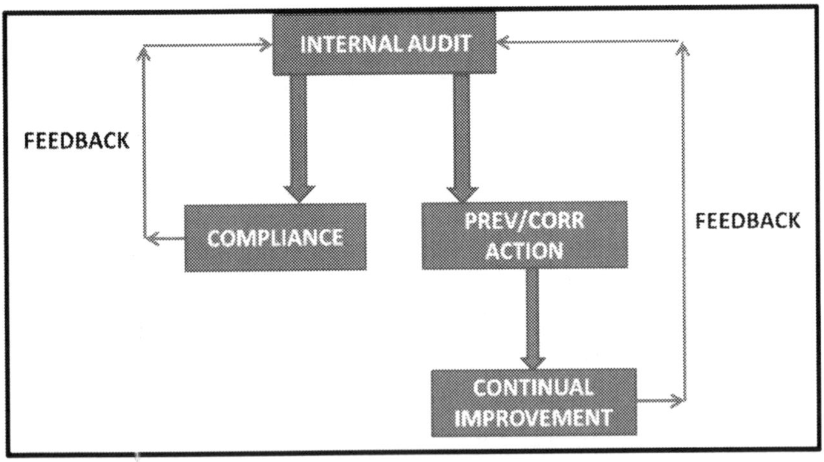

4. Auditing Process Measurement and Confirmation

Management can use findings from internal audits for measurement, analyses, and improvement of existing processes; and to ensure conformance to established standards, contract requirements, regulatory requirements, as well as achievement of top management goals and objectives (e.g., reducing hazardous waste). Modern quality management system auditing goes beyond the earlier quality system expectations, which focused on adherence to customer contract specifications through individual disciplines (e.g. purchasing, inventory control, statistical techniques, etc.), and end of pipeline inspections, rather than overall processes. Well-constructed internal process audits can measure conformance to customer requirements, but they can also check customer communication and feedback, and verify/validate the processes.

5. Auditing Strategic Planning

Executing strategic plans requires taking broad plans and policies and translating them into discrete, measurable, components. Internal auditing of the Strategic Plan evaluates the organization's progress in meeting those components. Policies with vague goals and objectives, or unquantifiable performance measurements, become "paper" policies, and lead to personnel discouragement, customer dissatisfaction, and organizational failure. Please look again at Chapter Two.

6. Auditing the Raising of Problems to Management Attention

Modern internal auditing assesses the day-to-day effectiveness of organizations in measurable terms (delivery dates, rejects, recycled material, unit costs, etc.). It spotlights specific practices or procedures which may require increased management attention. Human resources management audits evaluate personnel structure in terms of qualifications, training, numbers, and functions versus needs. Internal auditing helps to evaluate facilities (e.g. floor space, computer systems/LAN, heavy machinery, etc.) in terms of adequacy and conformance. All this is meaningless, however, if audit findings do not receive management attention and actionable corrections are not generated, executed, and validated.

Summary

The success of an organization is the sum of the effectiveness of management authority, responsibility, and accountability. They are, in turn, the sum of the manner in which management deals with the findings of the internal audits.

All of the parts of the organization's integrated management system present themselves for assessment in the internal audit.

A management consultant whose strengths lie not only in the application of structured skills but in *objectivity*, can effectively audit an organization, and also develop a team of auditors to conduct scheduled internal audits routinely, after he/she has gone on to other challenges.

I believe that providing a client with an effective self-audit program is my best contribution, because it keeps helping after I'm gone.

Chapter Four: Quality Management

> *"Many companies are facing serious losses and wastes as a result of deficiencies in the quality planning process."*
>
> J. M. Juran

Every organization needs a quality management system with measurable goals.

Don't even think about NOT having a quality management system. Most likely, you are making products in accordance with something supplied by the customer/client. I recommend that you create your own program and ensure that it reflects (or exceeds) what the customer/client wants. This applies to services as well as products. I highly recommend taking ISO 9000 and structuring your IMS to it and to your business. You will discover as most do, that this is not a burden, and <u>you are already doing most of what is needed to certify.</u>

1. Planning for quality goals

Some time ago, and for a long time before, larger-than-life quality pioneer Dr. J.M. Juran stressed the importance of meaningful quality *planning.* He said that a quality (management) program should reflect goals that are:

a) *Operational as to overall results.* Goals that "suboptimize" performance of various activities can easily damage overall performance.
b) *All-inclusive.* Activities for which goals have been set tend to have high priority, but at the expense of remaining activities.
c) *Maintainable.* Goals should be designed in modular fashion so that elements can be revised without extensive teardown.
d) *Economic.* The value of meeting the goals should be clearly greater than the cost of setting and administering them.

No less important is the list of criteria as perceived by those who are faced with meeting the goals. To those operating forces, goals should be:

a) *Legitimate.* Goals should have undoubted official status.
b) *Understandable.* They should be stated in clear, simple language, ideally in the language of those who are faced with meeting the goals.
c) *Applicable.* The goals should fit the conditions of use or should include the flexibility to adapt to conditions of use.
d) *Worthwhile.* Meeting the goal should be regarded as benefiting those who do the added work as well as benefiting the organization that established the goal.
e) *Attainable.* It should be possible for "ordinary" people to meet the goals by applying reasonable effort.
f) *Equitable.* Since performance against goals is frequently used for merit rating of individuals, the goals should be reasonably alike as to difficulty of attainment. [14]

---

[14] Juran, J.M., <u>Juran on Planning for Quality</u> (See References)

I was just getting comfortable in my first job after retiring from the U.S. Navy, as one of the technical directors at an excellent A&E firm in Arlington, VA. The President asked one day if I would like to take the lead in marketing ISO 9000 for our mother company in the U.K. and also implement it inside our company. In a flashback to my Navy days, I readily volunteered. I then walked back to my office wondering what in the hell ISO 9000 was, and when would I ever stop volunteering. I went to BORDERS and bought several books on ISO 9000. That was in 1995, and I have loved that Standard ever since, especially in its subsequent revisions.

Several years later, while doing an ISO 9000 certification audit of a small electronics manufacturer, I discovered a piece of test equipment in use that was about two months late for its annual calibration. Was that important? Possibly, the company made pacemakers! (Note: Please feel free to gasp, I did)

I currently audit and consult in ISO 9000, ISO 14000, ISO 27000, and ISO 28000. I love these standards because I see the need for them and have seen how much good they can do for an organization. I have also enjoyed combining them into an IMS and seeing my recommendations do some measurable good.

What is a Quality Management System?

A quality management system, or "QMS" starts out as a decision from top management that the product or service created by the organization will conform to (or exceed) customer requirements, while still achieving a benefit for the organization.

Next, the organization creates or gathers standards or specifications for its products or services, and the metrics needed to assess conformity with those standards or specifications.

Concurrently, subsystems develop that take the mission of the organization, break it down into processes, and marry the processes to the standards. Qualified personnel are assigned quality responsibilities and controls are added to the QMS, to ensure that the organization creates its products or services in accordance with the standards that it has determined to be the optimum, and subject to revision as necessary through a controlled process[15].

Wrap it all up in a documentation system made up of management tools in the form of concise but meaningful records and reports and you have everything you need.

Simple! Well, maybe.

The fastest way to tell you how to create an effective QMS if you have none, or the one you have isn't working is to take you quickly through ISO 9000 and strongly recommend that you consider implementing it in your organization. Whether you want to go all the way to Certification with it is up to you, but I also recommend that.

Table 4-1 contains (again) the basic requirements of an effective QMS in general and ISO 9000 in particular. These requirements are not unreasonable, but they are essential.

Table 4-1 Essentials of a Quality Management System

Requirement	Effective QMS	ISO 9000
Structured Standard and Explanation	X	X
Top Management Involvement	X	X
Employee Ownership	X	X
Risks identified	X	X
Reflected in Strategic Plan	X	X
Process Oriented	X	X
Resistance at first	X	X

---

[15] Please remember that "training" is not always "qualification".

Documentation required	X	X
Training and Qualification required	X	X
Manual and/or checklists or flowcharts for structure	X	X
Capable of self-audit	X	X
Consolidates other standards, specifications, and compliance requirements	X	X
Feedback loops established	X	X
Corrective and/or preventive action	X	X

How much of a quality management system do you need?

Now it is time to build the QMS. Our system, as noted above, is made up of subsystems, which in turn are made up of processes, elements, and activities – the objective of which is to allow the organization to make conforming products at competitive costs. Unlike *quality control* or *quality assurance* programs of the past, we are not trying to spot a non-conforming product at the end of the pipeline (when you either send it back for rework or throw it away), your QMS should monitor the processes and preclude making of non-conforming products; then move on, continuously improving.

Here are the clauses of the ISO 9000 International Quality Management System Standard. If your organization does not perform all of these operations (e.g. you don't design anything), you need to state that in the Quality Manual. [16]

Please review Table 4-2 and you'll see how many of these you are already doing. You may be doing more of them than you realized.

---

[16] ANSI/ISO/ASQ Q9001:2015. Contact the American Society for Quality at www.asq.org for it and some very good guidance on implementation.

Table 4.2 ISO 9001:2015 Clauses

ISO 9000 Clauses/ Sub-clauses	
1.	Scope
2.	Normative References
3.	Terms and Definitions
4.	Context of the Organization
4.1	Understanding the Organization and its context
4.2	Understanding the needs and expectations of interested parties
4.3	Determining the scope of the quality management system
4.4	Quality management system and its processes
5.	Leadership
5.1	Leadership and commitment
5.1.1	General
5.1.2	Customer focus
5.2	Policy
5.2.1	Developing the quality policy
5.2.2	Communicating the quality policy
5.3	Organizational roles, responsibilities, and authorities
6. Planning	
6.1	Actions to address risks and opportunities
6.2	Quality objectives and planning to achieve them
6.3	Planning of changes
7.	Support
7.1	Resources
7.1.1	General
7.1.2	People
7.1.3	Infrastructure
7.1.4	Environment for the operation of processes
7.1.5	Monitoring and measuring resources
7.1.5.1	General
7.1.5.2	Measurement traceability

ISO 9000 Clauses/ Sub-clauses	
7.1.6	Organizational knowledge
7.2	Competence
7.3	Awareness
7.4	Communication
7.5	Documented information
7.5.1	General
7.5.2	Creation and updating
7.5.3	Control of documented information
8	Operation
8.1	Operational planning and control
8.2	Requirements for products and services
8.2.1	Customer communication
8.2.2	Determining the requirements related to products and services
8.2.3	Review of requirements related to products and services
8.2.4	Changes to requirements for products and services
8.3	Design and development of products and services
8.3.1	General
8.3.2	Design and development planning
8.3.3	Design and development inputs
8.3.4	Design and development controls
8.3.5	Design and development outputs
8.3.6	Design and development changes
8.4	Control of externally provided processes, products, and services
8.4.1	General
8.4.2	Type and extent of control
8.4.3	Information for external providers
8.5	Production and service provision
8.5.1	Control of production and service provision
8.5.2	Identification and traceability
8.5.3	Property belonging to customers or external providers

ISO 9000 Clauses/ Sub-clauses	
8.5.4	Preservation
8.5.5	Post-delivery activities
8.5.6	Control of changes
8.6	Release of products or services
8.7	Control of nonconforming outputs
9.	Performance evaluation
9.1.1	General
9.1.2	Customer satisfaction
9.1.3	Analysis and evaluation
9.2	Internal audit
9.3	Management review
9.3.1	General
9.3.2	Management review inputs
9.3.3	Management review outputs
10.	Improvement
10.1	General
10.2	Nonconformity and corrective action
10.3	Continual improvement

Again, you may not have to do all of them. However, if there are elements that you are not doing that you should, this would be a good time to structure (or re-structure) a complete quality management system. If some of what you have read is completely new to you, then you probably will need some help.

The fastest way to build a complete and effective QMS, in my opinion, is to go with ISO 9000. Again, go to the website I mentioned. You can download the Standard right then and there.

Summary

Every organization needs a quality management system or "QMS". The best way I know to develop a comprehensive QMS quickly is to implement ISO 9000 and the best way to implement ISO 9000 is as part of an integrated management system. You can implement it just for yourself or you can go for certification.

You'll be surprised at how many of the requirements you are doing already. You may also be surprised by how much you are NOT doing.

Chapter Five: Environmental Management

CEO Note: Never mind "Global Warming" and "Climate Change"; focus your environmental management strategy on Pollution Prevention and Energy Conservation. Make real, quantifiable improvements to real, quantifiable operations. If we all do our best to minimize pollution and to conserve energy, the polar bears will be just fine, thank you.

Points to Remember

✓ Environmental *management* is better than environmental *compliance.*

✓ Every organization, large or small, public or private needs to practice pollution prevention and energy conservation.

✓ ISO 14000 provides all the structure and guidance needed, and can be a highly valuable part of an IMS.

Unstructured environmental management programs that sprung from external compliance mandates were often considered "add-on" programs and held separate and distinct from an organization's day-to-day operations. Environmental personnel were in staff positions, often charged solely with handling all the compliance-related reporting and without authority to correct environmentally unsafe situations. They were perpetually *reactive*, instead of *proactive*. Aggressively improving the environmental posture of an organization usually came immediately before (or immediately after) a visit from local environmental regulators.

The International Environmental Management System Standard ISO 14000 was first introduced in 1996. Certification to this Standard forced environmental management into the Board Room, by (1) requiring incorporation of environmental planning into an organization's strategic plan; (2) making an organization identify all the environmental aspects of its operations; and (3) requiring a risk management program, wherein those same environmental aspects undergo nearly continuous evaluation with regard to the threats, criticalities, and vulnerabilities associated with their existence.[17]

Also, and you know this, an environmental management program must have the total support and involvement of all levels of management, as well as all stakeholders. This chapter discusses the proper mindset for environmental management, some thought provokers, and what a structured, professional, and effective environmental management program should look like.

Do what is recommended in the pages that follow, and you will have everything you need, and possibly not a moment too soon.

If you think having an environmental management program is expensive, try <u>not</u> having one.

---

[17] See the appendix on Risk Management.

> *About fifteen years ago, while on a project to assess the impact of environmental regulations on U.S. shipyards, I was part of a team that traveled to a number of shipbuilding yards and ship repair facilities along the East, Gulf, and West coasts. One East coast yard production manager floated us out on a veritable sea of tears because it cost him great sums of money to haul expended sandblast grit (and embedded paint chips) to a landfill. Faced with the same predicament, an executive in another yard told me of the deal he had made with a local road contractor to sell his grit for use in road building. He didn't make much, but he <u>saved</u> a great deal. That same executive then described a costly capital investment he was planning, and how he had figured his break-even point and how he knew when the equipment would start paying for itself.*
>
> *Moral: Think environmental <u>management</u>, not environmental <u>compliance</u>.*

The right environmental management mindset

Whether you run a giant manufacturing conglomerate or sit at a computer in your home office (like I do now), you can be an environmental titan and a hero to the grandkids. How? First, by wrapping your managerial mind and leadership skills around twelve thoughts I am about to present to you. Then, after you have the right mindset, we'll structure an environmental management system[18].

1. You cannot pursue sustainable development for your organization without an environmental management program, and that must have strong roots in pollution prevention.
2. Environmental *Compliance* is not Environmental *Management*. You are not in charge when you are in compliance. It is only when you have an effective

---

[18] God gave us ten, Woodrow Wilson fourteen. I'm right in the middle.

environmental management program in your organization that you are not only compliant, but ethical, responsible, profitable, self-sustaining, and the best neighbor possible.

3. People think (not inappropriately) that no single action on their part will make a significant improvement to the environmental condition. Are they right or wrong? Yes! I mean that if everyone does everything he/she can, both at home and at work, there will be measurable improvements. The reason that this does not sell is that it is not a scare tactic.

4. Technically complex environmental problems seem to outnumber simple, effective mitigations. This leads to public confusion, frustration, discouragement, and (eventually) apathy.

5. Environmental strategies complement each other. Reducing the amount of pollutants generated reduces the complexity of the recycling or disposal effort. Also, conserving energy reduces pollution (e.g., less exhaust gas).

6. Environmental strategies produce opportunities for cost avoidance. For example initiatives such as "going paperless" or recycling office paper reduces not only waste, but the cost of disposing of it. Conserving energy lowers operating costs. [19]

7. Effective pollution prevention begins with the realization that there is no single all-encompassing solution to environmental problems. Rather, we need to identify all the problems, and then identify a broad spectrum of preventive and corrective measures, looking always for synergies, wherein one action solves or mitigates more than one problem[20].

8. Effective pollution prevention can mean technologically improving a process, or it can mean just not doing the

---

[19] In 1989, implementing those two initiatives in an administration building I was responsible for reduced our dumpster requirements by two thirds. This was considerable cost avoidance over an annual recording period.

[20] See the discussion on Synergy.

process at all. Simply reducing the number of times you do something (or not doing it anymore) does not require a big research and development budget, and it can make a measurable improvement.

9. Every business venture has an environmental cost, so keep looking until you find it. Don't assume that because something is environmentally "friendly" that there is no cost or that it could not be done better. Environmentally friendly practices may have a reduced impact, but there is still an impact. Look at every action or process to determine if it is necessary. That's just good business and smart managers will embrace pollution prevention as an opportunity as well as a requirement.

10. When dealing with an environmental problem in your home or organization, look to see if it is "front end" or "back end". For instance: conserving resources is done at the front end; recycling waste is done at the back end. See below.

11. Physical waste is not only an environmental problem that must be dealt with; it is a waste of an organization's time and resources.

12. Recycling pollutant material is good, but not creating it in the first place is better.

Front end vs. back end resource conservation

In *Prosperity without Pollution – the Prevention Strategy for Industry and Consumers,* authors Joel Hirschhorn and Kirsten Oldenburg[21] identify front end and back end pollution. Energy conservation is a good example of protecting resources at the front end, while waste management operations typify actions at the back end. The authors focus their readers on the importance focusing first on the front end; i.e., don't use the resource (or as much of it) in the first place. If you give appropriate attention to the front end, not only will you accomplish a great deal, but back end challenges will be easier.

---

[21] See the Reference Section.

Another example: the manufacture and use of *packaging materials* is a front end cost and a user of resources; the disposal of the packaging after they have been used is a back end cost and results in more waste for disposal. Always consider packaging when you are looking for opportunities to reduce your pollution footprint.

Pollution Prevention

Table 5-1 contains some representative pollution prevention challenges and solutions that you can apply both at home and in your organization. Look at them, and as you do, you will think of many others.

Table 5-1 Pollution Prevention challenges and solutions for CEOs

Challenge	Solutions/Mitigations
Reduce damage/ destruction of the Ozone layer	Replace ozone depleting substances (e.g., Freon) with safe substitutes.
Reduce air pollution	Use alternative fuels where possible; conserve energy
Reduce hazardous waste	Change manufacturing processes[22]; Buy products that neither require nor create hazardous or toxic materials
Reduce acid rain	Substitute low sulfur coal in power plants Substitute renewable energy sources

---

[22] Hazardous materials with longer shelf lives do not have to be discarded as frequently.

Reduce smog	Replace existing vehicles with hybrid or natural gas vehicles; Allow personnel to work from home routinely or occasionally; Encourage use of public transportation; Operate private and public vehicles more economically (e.g., properly inflate tires, replace air filters, drive slowly) Replace products containing volatile organic compounds (e.g., propellants with pump sprayers)
Reduce trash and garbage (toxic and non-toxic)	Replace toxic products with non-toxic products and products with greater durability; Replace products having excessive packaging
Reduce groundwater contamination	Replace inappropriate fertilizers and/or pesticides, or reduce their use
Reduce potential lead poisoning	Eliminate lead soldering in piping and/or food containers
Reduce exposure to dioxin in consumables	Procure no-bleached products (e.g., replace white paper coffee filters with brown paper or mesh screens.

Now you have the idea. Make up your own table of environmental challenges and solutions for your own home or organization.

You don't have to change the world, just your little piece of it. The doctrine of *continual improvement,* which we discuss throughout this book should lead you to the belief that no process or practice is indispensable or cannot be improved.

In Pollution Prevention, it is usually better to eliminate a process entirely than to improve it.

I don't mean to imply that pollution prevention at your level is automatic, always meaningful, or simple. Instead, look at your processes, procedures, and practices (even those that are already environmentally friendly and popular), ask the following questions and be the judge:

- Have you identified all the waste or pollutant outputs of your operations or processes?
- Are these processes/operations absolutely necessary?
- Is there an equivalent process in existence that does not pollute, or pollutes to a lesser degree?
- Has there been an effort to identify a substitute process or product?
- Is there a financial benefit from the current process or product and who receives this benefit?

Recycling is good – prevention is better

By now, most of you (even if you work from home, like me) are into some form of recycling program. That's good. However, it's better not to procure or generate the waste in the first place, for reasons like these:

- The pollutants produced by recycling paper are greater than those generated in the original (i.e., virgin) paper making process. Go "paperless" when you can.
- Recycling waste oil creates additional pollutants.
- Despite the recycler's best efforts, not all recyclable material is rescued from the waste streams. Many of those plastic water bottles go into the landfills, along with the rest of the regular trash and garbage.
- The recycling processes themselves often create their own pollution. Many SUPERFUND sites started out as recycling facilities.

ISO 14000 – International Environmental Management Standard

CEO Note: ISO 14000 is the quintessential standard for environmental management systems. I discuss it almost exclusively in this chapter because it has something for any and every organization, and what it creates are management tools, not recurring reports.

ISO 14000 (like the other ISO Standards) is based on the principle of Continuous Improvement, shown in figure 5-1, and methodology known as Plan-Do-Check-Act, or PDCA, described as follows:

Plan: Establish the objectives and processes necessary to deliver results in accordance with the organization's environmental policy.

Do: Implement the processes.

Check: Monitor and measure the processes against environmental policy, objectives, targets, legal, and other requirements and report the results.

Act: Take actions to continually improve the performance of the environmental management system.

Environmental Aspects

An "environmental aspect is: "An element of an organization's activities or products or services with the potential to impact the environment. A significant environmental aspect has or can have significant environmental impact."

Table 5-2 and figure 5-1 both describe the identification and tracking of typical environmental aspects. Management needs to monitor its environmental aspects and look for opportunities to reduce or eliminate environmental risk in its operations.

Table 5-2 Environmental aspect tracking and risk assessment (notional)

Number	Process	Aspect	Location	Threat	Criticality	Vulnerability	Risk	Course of Action	Revised Vulnerability	Revised Risk
EA 1	Ship refueling	Oil Spill; Harbor Pollution; Fire	Terminal	4	7	6	168	Daytime Only/Oil Boom/Fire boats	4	112
EA 2	Cargo Loading/Offloading	Oil Spill; Harbor Pollution; Fire	Terminal	6	7	7	294	Daytime Only/Oil Boom/Fire boats	5	210
EA 3	Equipment Op/Maint.	Oil/HAZMAT Spill	Terminal	4	7	5	140	Absorbent Matting	4	112
EA4	Dry Cargo Movement	Breakage/Debris	Terminal	3	6	5	90	Daytime Only	4	72
EA5	Compressed gas handling	Explosion/Fire	Terminal	4	6	6	144	Responders on station	5	120
EA 6	Container Movement	Drop/breakage/HAZMAT/Deb ris	Terminal	4	3	6	72	Responders on station	5	60
EA 7	Ship Transit	Collision/Grounding/Fire/Oil Spill	Harbor/Restricted Waters	4	9	6	216	Responders on station	4	144
EA 8	Ship Transit	Collision/Grounding/Fire/Oil Spill	Open Ocean	3	9	5	135	Responders on station	4	108

Figure 5-1 The risk assessment in table 5-2 shown graphically

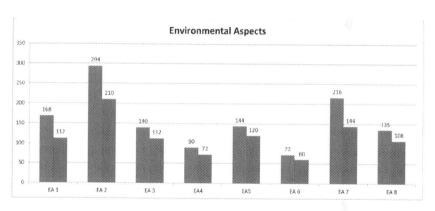

Like the other international standards, ISO 14000 is intended to provide organizations with a comprehensive, replicable, and responsive system overseeing the development of policies, procedures, and processes, not only to meet legal and regulatory requirements, but to ensure the required economic development of the organization.

Also like the other international standards, ISO 14000 gets into your strategic plan, by requiring you to identify your environmental *aspects*, and incorporate their management into your environmental policies, goals, and objectives. Moreover, it requires you to develop viable and consistent risk assessment, management review, and self-auditing capabilities.

The Standard is not a "standard" for product or service performance, and does not establish acceptable values, as for emissions, pollutants, or other levels of acceptability.

Here are the clauses of the ISO 14000 Environmental Quality Management System Standard.[23]

Please review table 5-3 and you'll see how many of these you are already doing. You may be doing more of them than you realize. Most people are.

Table 5-3 ISO14000 Clauses

ISO 14000 Clause/Sub clause	Title
1.	Scope
2.	Normative references
3.	Terms and definitions
4.	Context of the organization
4.1	Understanding the organization and its context
4.2	Understanding the needs and expectations of interested parties
4.3	Determining the scope of the EMS
4.4	Environmental management system
5.	Leadership
5.1	Leadership and commitment
5.2	Environmental policy
5.3	Organizational roles, responsibilities, and authorities
6.	Planning
6.1	Actions to address risks and opportunities
6.1.1	Risks and opportunities
6.1.2	Environmental aspects
6.1.3	Compliance obligations
6.1.4	Planning action

---

[23] ANSI/ISO/ASQ 14001:2015. Contact the American Society for Quality at www.asq.org for it and some very good guidance on implementation.

ISO 14000 Clause/Sub clause	Title
6.2	Environmental objectives and planning to achieve them
7	Support
7.1	Resources
7.2	Competence
7.3	Awareness
7.4	Communication
7.5	Documented information
8.	Operation
8.1	Operational planning and control
8.2	Emergency preparedness and response
9.	Performance evaluation
9.1	Monitoring, measurement, analysis, and evaluation
9.2	Internal audit
9.3	Management review
10	Improvement
10.1	General
10.2	Nonconformity and corrective action
10.3	Continual improvement

Figure 5-2 outlines the structure of an OP for an integrated management system.

Figure 5-2 The structure of the IMS

A Certification to the ISO 14000 International Standard from an authorized registrar reinforces an organization's credibility with governments, stakeholders, customers, and neighbors, not to mention providing an excellent basis for justifiable bragging.

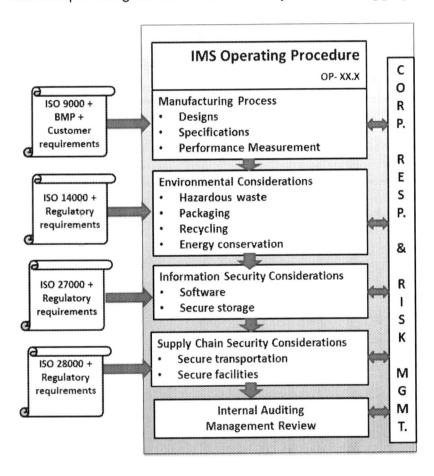

Summary

This chapter discussed the importance of an effective environmental management system to any organization, and how well it fits into an IMS.

Adding an ISO 14000-compliant section to an ISO 9000-compliant operating procedure (OP) can satisfy the requirements of both International Standards and create a comprehensive OP for your IMS.

Chapter Six: Information Management - Get In Front of This and Stay There

✓ Organizations must factor Information Technology (IT) into all of their missions, but, IT should not be and end in itself, nor should it have its own set of missions.

✓ Managing IT is no different from and other business component. Establish your policies, goals, and risk parameters; implement, train, measure, and benchmark. And then, audit, audit, audit.

✓ IT auditing must also address the *security* of your IT systems

✓ Auditing IT systems only to ensure compliance with customer requirements just perpetuates the status quo. Generating preventive and corrective actions during those audits, and reassessing your goals based on audit findings, perpetuate continual improvement and help to guarantee a robust information security posture into the future.

This chapter discusses some of the differences between discreet and disparate information technology operations and those same operations coordinated and "synergized" under an information management system.

Several years ago, I worked as a Military Analyst for the Department of Defense on programs that included (like all modern Defense programs) *Information Warfare.* The lesson I continually re-learned during that time was that:

Information is the only "weapon" that can be
in more than one place at the same time

This is a lesson not just for the Department of Defense, but for any organization intent on getting in front, staying in front, and protecting itself and its people. Easy? Of course not!

But, however great the challenge, IT has tremendous potential that experienced auditors or managers can recognize and exploit. The opportunities for continual improvement are as limitless as cyberspace.

The paragraphs that follow will cover how information technology, even in its most advanced state can be managed and protected inside an integrated management system, and how anything less jeopardizes the existence of the organization, the capability of management, and the effectiveness of the auditing process.

Here are ten auditable areas in which organizations can create and sustain (and auditors can verify) credible, effective, and secure information management systems.

1. Managing Information Technology

To *manage* information technology is to manage a myriad of diverse systems and components, all (hopefully) working in the service of the organization, and not of just working for themselves. IT is often considered a "black art" by the other departments, who only think about it when something goes wrong. Inputs and requirements come from all directions, often with the biggest fear being that "Sales" will commit to something that IT cannot deliver. In fact, there may be no coordination or dialogue between IT and the other departments. IT folks (e.g., help desks) may just handle what flashes across their screens, having little understanding or appreciation for the mission and goals of the organization and the roles that they play; their battle cry being: "Did you try re-booting?" Big help!

Auditing of typical IT management likely uncovers:

- Poor organization of the IT staff;
- Poor coordination with the other departments;
- Lack of clearly defined roles and responsibilities;
- Gaps and overlaps, with some functions or processes having more than one overseer and other functions or processes ignored entirely; and (worst of all)
- Lack of individual accountability.

These problems, when left "un-audited", undiscovered, and uncorrected inevitably lead to:

- Customer dissatisfaction, despite the best efforts of the other departments
- Budget problems (e.g., waste and shortfalls)
- Staffing problems, including employee turnover, ineffective training, and low morale.
- A general ineffectiveness of processes, thereby requiring longer run times, increased oversight, and (in some form) re-work
- A systems "crash".

In many ways, IT is no different from any other function in its need to be integrated into the organization. As auditors, we often see problems when Sales, Marketing, Design, or (worst of all) R&D operate in their own orbits. However, the introduction of advanced, high speed systems and equipment can separate IT's orbit even further from that of the organization, and control and management are profoundly challenged.

Table 6-1 contrasts managing discreet information technology areas with managing those same areas as part of an integrated management system.

Table 6-1 Discreet IT Operations vs. an Integrated Management System

Auditable Area	Separate, Discreet Operations	IT in an Integrated Management System
1. Information Technology Management	More easily duplicated by competitors; synergies not identified; customer requirements not always clear	Process approach; synergies, competitive advantages identified/ optimized; flexible, sustainable
2. Budgeting and Provisioning of Resources	Resources spread over multiple projects; accountability not clear	Key issues tracked, understood, funded; accountability clear
3. Systems Training	Multiple, possibly conflicting requirements; Loss of accountability	Standardized and centralized; "qualifications" defined; Accountabilities clear and assigned
4. Internal Auditing	Multiple platforms, issues, operations, accountabilities; focused on compliance	Clear, traceable accountability Preventive/corrective actions developed; follow-up
5 Policies and Objectives	Many issues, some not addressed; disparate	Ownerships, targets, accountabilities well defined; shared, consistent, credible
6. Emergency Planning	Spans multiple platforms and operations; uncoordinated responses	Operational impacts/ responsibilities clearly defined
7. Risk Management	Multiple platforms, multiple assessments	System assessed holistically, risks/ mitigations identified holistically

8. Performance Measurement	Issues/targets not all tracked, or tracked separately	Specific, measurable targets; organization-wide, tracked centrally
9. Governance	Limited accountability; IT-specific; detached	Scope, accountability defined Organization-aligned
10. Continual Improvement	Multiple platforms, undefined performance	Scopes, targets, measurement defined; measurable, predictable improvement.

2. Budgeting and Provision of Resources

The success of the organization's IT is the direct result of the IT Manager/CIO's ability to operate in a fiscally sound manner. It is easier to do this if IT is handled holistically in a *process approach* and as part of an overall integrated management system

Segregated or detached approaches to IT budgeting and resource allocation often lead to:

- Frequent revision of the funding requirements due to transitory changes in markets, technologies, or operations
- Lack of coordination with other departments (e.g., Sales, Production, or Shipping)
- Incompatible system components
- An incomplete risk management process, wherein not all parameters are defined (see below)
- Technical requirements not reflecting or aligning with organization or strategic requirements
- Inadvertent departure from legal or regulatory requirements due to lack of communication and staffing
- Loss of control or accountability.

3. Systems Training

Both centralized and decentralized information systems contain large numbers of routine and repetitive tasks for which operators require training. However, in a centralized approach, those same tasks are part of an integrated management system, and can be standardized – the benefits of that standardization being:

- Improved quality and consistency
- End-user as well as operator training
- Reduced training costs, operating costs, and cost/unit of productivity (e.g., forms/hour)
- Objective measurement standards
- Objective, defensible performance evaluations
- Defensible staffing requests and budgets.

Operations that are ideal for standardization and *qualification* of designated personnel include (but are not limited to):

- Data backup and recovery
- System startups, shutdowns, and resets
- Invoice generation, processing, and follow-up
- Payrolls
- System changes or upgrades; capacity management
- Audits and verifications; branch office support
- Troubleshooting and help desks
- System security (protection against unauthorized use, hacking, loss/theft/destruction of data)
- Network administration; asset, bandwidth, and configuration management
- Monitoring and license compliance
- Trend and history reporting.

> _**CEO Note:**_ _You should not audit IT processes just to ensure compliance. You should audit to find better and more secure ways to operate, if you want to get the most from IT auditing._

4. Internal Auditing of Information Management

Auditing for its own sake accomplishes little, except to waste resources. I have found, in my journeys, that some organizations internally audit their IT processes only to ensure *compliance* with customer requirements. More wasteful still, customers expend time and travel funds by sending in their own auditors to audit the same processes as do the internal auditors.[24] The press (and stress) of checking a myriad of small, repetitive, functions, as you can do in IT, can cause operators and auditors not to think about and pursue potential ways to do something better[25]. We discuss Continual Improvement throughout this book; but for now *it's only important to remember that audit findings should generate preventive and corrective actions.* Preventive actions are actions which, when taken, preclude the *occurrence* of defects or nonconformities. Corrective actions, when taken, preclude the *recurrence* of defects or nonconformities. Likely areas for the identification of IT preventive and corrective actions include:

- Help desks
- End-user support
- Network administration
- Systems administration
- Applications testing and management
- Database administration
- Applications interface
- Business analysis.

Unlike only ensuring compliance, auditing to generate, implement, and evaluate preventive and corrective actions can have a positive and measurable impact on long term

---

[24] Ideally, certification to ISO 27000, Information Security Management Systems optimally structures internal and certification/surveillance audits for organizations, reducing or eliminating the need for customer audits. Read the Standard if you have not already read it.

[25] Remember this old favorite: *"Better is the enemy of good enough"?*

productivity. That is, the organization can produce more, with the same or a smaller expenditure of labor or capital.

Figure 6-1 summarizes the generation of "actionable" findings and the importance of feedback loops.

Figure 6-1 Productive IT Auditing

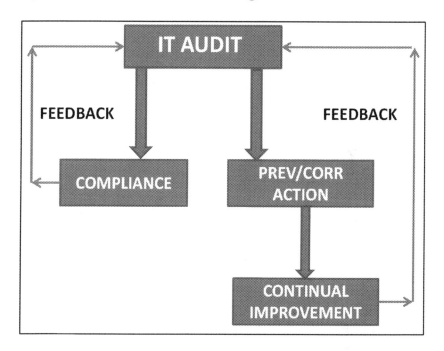

5. Policies and Objectives

An organization's policies and objectives, as they pertain to IT, must address IT as a part of the overall mission and framework of that organization. Otherwise, IT would exist for itself (as is often the case), and, in doing so:

- IT requirements, capabilities, and potential for contribution would not be seen in terms of overall organizational benefit
- IT requirements from other departments would literally "never see the light of day"

- Responsibilities and accountabilities would not be identified
- Comprehensive metrics would not be established, nor would there be actionable targets and milestones. There would be no groundwork or mindset for continual improvement
- Top management support and visibility may not be established or maintained. IT's impact on the entire organization would not be constantly seen and monitored
- IT risk (and the attendant threats, criticalities, and vulnerabilities) may not be developed or aligned with those of the entire organization
- IT performance may not be measured in terms of contribution to the entire organization.

IT policies must, in fact, be *organizational* policies because they must deal with (to mention a few):

- Security and security incidents
- Data collected and stored
- Customer information
- Internet, main, and instant messaging usage
- Records management
- Legal and regulatory requirements
- Training and Human Resource Management.

6. Emergency Planning

NFPA 1600: Standard on Disaster/Emergency Planning Management and Business Continuity Programs (2010 Ed.) identified five basic plans that organizations are expected to have ready to execute.[26]

The first is the Strategic Plan, and we all know about those. The four other plans that organizations need to understand and implement are summarized in table 6-2.

---

[26] The National Fire Protection Association; learn more at www.nfpa.org.

Table 6-2 Emergency Plans

Plan	Purpose
Emergency Operations Response Plan	Assigns functional responsibilities for emergency actions
Mitigation Plan	Establishes short and long range reduction/ elimination of hazards
Recovery Plan	Identifies strategies and priorities for restoration of facilities, services, or programs
Continuity Plan	Identifies critical functions that must be maintained during recovery

The effectiveness (and indeed, success) of these plans in an IT organization requires the *centralized* control and management of all the information system components. That is, they all need to be part of the Information Management System, and not free-standing components of the user departments.

An organization in which information management in general and/or IT in particular is decentralized among different user departments results in incomplete plans, multiple plans, or no plans at all, as the different departments struggle with issues dealing with responsibility and accountability. This is unacceptable in an emergency, and seasoned auditors and managers already know that.

7. Risk Management

I write about risk management throughout this book. I won't duplicate any of the graphs and tables, but will instead just remind the reader that:

- Each organization must identify its appropriate balance of risk and reward.
- Organizations and the decisions that they reach are unique, and each carries with it a host of variables. Accordingly, organizations need to develop general skills to assess and manage risk and return in each of the unique situations and decisions.

- The organization's risk management process (and the general skills used in it), in whatever form that it takes, must include:

  - Defining parameters (e.g., threats, criticalities, and vulnerabilities)
  - Data collection to address those parameters
  - Reaching conclusions and acting on them
  - Evaluating the results of the actions taken.

Management must determine the amount of risk that they are willing to live with, and auditors (like us) should ensure that the risk management process effectively "informs" the decisions that are ultimately made.

8. Performance Measurement

A robust program of IT performance measurement aligns IT in a credible way the over-arching organization goals and objectives. Business unit leaders in the organization see not only the alignment, but its "greater good" recompenses in the form of improved performance, greater productivity, competitive advantage, and increased market share. Performance measurement adds value when data is collected and analyzed, actions are taken, and the results of the actions are compared with the original condition.

Performance measurement programs understandably vary with the functions and missions of the organization. There are, however, some common tasks for nearly all performance measurement programs. For example:

- Defining the IT "dashboard" (i.e., defining what you want to measure and receiving immediate feedback)
- Conducting baseline surveys
- Developing analysis and reporting processes
- Developing metrics
- Structuring and implementing a management program, to include:

- Reassessment and follow-up
- Periodic reviews and "stress tests".

> *The ability to perform benchmarking and gap analysis, that is, to determine where you are as opposed to where you should be, is as important when working with IT operations as with any others normally found in business or industry.*

9. Governance

Governance, for our purposes, means the strategy that Management employs to ensure that IT successfully executes its operations in support of the organization's strategic and tactical plans, goals, and objectives. In its execution, governance often requires the establishment of a "steering committee": senior department/business unit members under the Chief Information Officer (CIO).

Functions of a steering committee normally include:

- Alignment and approval of IT priorities, objectives, and direction
- Removal or impediments and "disconnects"
- Approval of IT funding, projects, and related expenditures
- Adherence to legal and regulatory requirements
- Development, approval, and implementation of audit and performance standards
- Oversight/review of security practices and controls
- IT architecture and configuration management
- Senior level support and advocacy
- Ensuring IT accountability to the rest of the organization.

Is it all worth the effort? Very much so in my experience! IT governance under a CIO and steering committee can be expected to benefit the organization because:

- The entire organization provides input and feedback on decisions, priorities, and expenditures
- Increased scrutiny of operations enhances and supports long term goals and efficiency
- Departments/business units gain access and representation. They also gain a better understanding of all IT priorities and how they are linked
- The CIO benefits from the direct feedback of the other business units.

10. Continual Improvement

Many of the specifics that sustain continual improvement have been covered already. The decision to establish policies, goals and objectives, develop metrics, and to implement a robust, credible, audit process, undoubtedly supports continual improvement. However, the perpetuation of these component parts synergistically requires (as mentioned before) a Continual Improvement *mindset*. Management must not only resolve to continue performing these component parts, but also to continue increasing their effectiveness, which improves not only the effectiveness of the information management system but that of the entire organization. That's continual improvement.

Summary

Information *Technology* becomes Information *Management* when an organization incorporates IT into its overall management strategy; contributing to, and having accountability in, all of the organization's missions. Successful implementation and operation in accordance with this strategy can be expected to result in:

- Improved customer service
- More efficient allocation of resources
- Improved system performance and uptime
- Reduction of risk
- Increased system and staff productivity
- Improved morale
- Sustained, ever improving organization performance and security.

Information management, now made robust internally, takes its place as an essential part of the organization's Integrated Management System.

The pages that follow contain an information *security* checklist.

Information Security Management System Checklist (Ref: ISO 27000)

4.1 General requirements

❑ Is an Information Security Management System maintained for ensuring that products conform to requirements?

❑ Is the Information Security Management System properly documented?

❑ Does the organization:
  ○ Identify processes needed for the ISMS
  ○ Determine process sequence and interaction
  ○ Determine the criteria and methods necessary to ensure effective operation and control of processes
  ○ Ensure resource and information necessary to support operation and monitoring of the processes
  ○ Monitor, measure, and analyze processes
  ○ Implement actions necessary to achieve the planned results and continual improvement of these processes?

❑ Are the processes managed by the organization in accordance with the International Standard?

4.2 Documentation requirements

4.2.1 General

❏ Does Information Security Management System documentation include documented statements of quality policies and quality objectives?
❏ Does documentation include documentation needed to ensure the effective planning, operation, and control of the processes?
❏ Are quality policies accumulated in a quality manual?
❏ Are documentation procedures in accordance with this International Standard?

4.2.2 Information Security & Risk Management Manual

❏ Is the Information Security & Risk Management Manual a controlled document?
❏ Does the quality manual include the following:
  ○ The scope of the Information Security Management System, including details of and justification for any exclusions?
  ○ The organization's type and size
  ○ The complexity and interaction of the organization's processes
  ○ The competence of the organization's personnel
  ○ Identification of quality controls
  ○ Production compatibility
  ○ Updating testing procedures
  ○ Identification of measurement requirements
  ○ Clarification of process and product requirements, and
  ○ Preparation of quality records?
  ○ A description of the interaction between the processes of the Information Security Management System?

❏ Does the organization measure, monitor, and analyze the processes established, and implement actions to ensure continuous improvement?

4.2.3 Control of documents

- ❑ Is there a documented procedure established to define the controls needed to:
  - ○ Approve documents for adequacy prior to issue
  - ○ Review and update as necessary and re-approve documents
  - ○ Ensure that changes and the current revision status of documents are identified
  - ○ Ensure that relevant versions of applicable documents are available at points of use
  - ○ Ensure that documents remain legible and identifiable
  - ○ Ensure that documents of external origin are identified and their distribution controlled
  - ○ Prevent the unintended use of obsolete documents, and to apply suitable identification to them if they are retained for any purpose?

- ❑ Are design- and quality-related documents controlled?
- ❑ Are documents reviewed and approved by authorized personnel?
- ❑ Are quality documents available to appropriate parties?
- ❑ Are obsolete documents removed from use?
- ❑ Is there an approved distribution list for documents?
- ❑ Are changes to documents reviewed and approved by the same personnel initiating the documents?
- ❑ Are changes to designs and documents properly reviewed?
- ❑ Are changes identified on engineering drawings?
- ❑ Is there a master list for controlling documents?
- ❑ Are documents reissued after changes have been made?

4.2.4 Control of records

- ❑ Are records established and maintained to provide evidence of conformity to requirements and of

the effective operation of the Information Security Management System?
- ❏ Do records remain legible, readily identifiable, and retrievable?
- ❏ Is there a documented procedure established to define the controls needed for the identification, storage, protection, retrieval, retention time, and disposition of records?
- ❏ Do records provide confidence that processes and resulting products conform?
- ❏ Are results of reviews and follow-up actions recorded?
- ❏ Do records indicate that reviews are conducted at suitable stages of design, development, and follow-up?
- ❏ Are the results of changes, verifications recorded?
- ❏ Are the results of subcontractor evaluations recorded?
- ❏ Are the results of calibrations recorded?
- ❏ Are there procedures for identifying, collecting, controlling, and storing quality records?
- ❏ Are quality documents and records accurate and current?
- ❏ Are the records of subcontractors and subcontractors' subcontractors accurate and current?
- ❏ Are quality records accessible?
- ❏ Are quality records retained for a sufficient amount of time?
- ❏ Are quality records available to the customer and other interested parties?

5.0 Management Responsibility

5.1 Management commitment

- ❏ Is top management actively involved in the Information Security Management System?
- ❏ Are quality policies, objectives, and plans developed?
- ❏ Is a Risk Assessment/Risk Management procedure developed?
- ❏ Does quality planning include the following:

- ○ Information Security Management System processes
- ○ Necessary resources?

5.2 Resource Management

❑ Has Management determine the resources it needs to:

❑ Establish, implement, monitor, review, maintain, and improve the ISMS;

❑ Ensure that information security procedures support the business requirements;

❑ Identify and address legal and regulatory requirements and contractual security obligations;

❑ Maintain adequate security by correct application of all implemented controls;

❑ Carry out reviews when necessary, and to react appropriately to the results of those reviews; and

❑ Where required, improve the effectiveness of the ISMS?

❑ Does top management ensure that customer security requirements are determined and are met with the aim of enhancing customer satisfaction?

5.2.2 Training, Awareness, and Competence

Are training needs and competencies identified?

❑ Are training resources adequate for the internal training needs?

❑ Are all personnel trained in quality technologies?

❑ Are training records maintained?

❑ Do training records include personnel:
- ○ Education
- ○ Experience
- ○ Training
- ○ Qualifications?

- ❑ Do personnel understand the relevance and importance of what they do and how they contribute to the achievement of quality objectives?
- ❑ Does the organization evaluate the effectiveness of the training provided?
- ❑ Does the organization define "competency" and how personnel can demonstrate competency within the Information Security Management System?

5.5.2 Security Officer

- ❑ Has a Security Officer(s) been appointed?
- ❑ (Irrespective of other duties) Does the Security Officer have the authority and responsibility to promote awareness of customer requirements throughout the organization?
- ❑ Are sufficient records maintained of organization and management quality activities?

5.5.3 Internal communication

- ❑ Does communication take place between various levels and functions regarding the effectiveness of the Information Security Management System?

6 Internal ISMS Audits

- ❑ Does the organization have and Internal ISMS Audit procedure and does it:
  - ○ Conform to the requirements of the International Standard and relevant legislation or regulations;
  - ○ Conform to the identified information security requirements;
  - ○ Are effectively implemented and maintained; and
  - ○ Perform as expected?

- ❑ Are all ISMS-related processes and procedures audited at least once per year?

7 Management Review of the ISMS

7.1 General

❑ Are management reviews scheduled at planned intervals to ensure continuing suitability, adequacy, and effectiveness?

7.2 Review input

❑ Do management reviews include:
  ○ Results of the ISMS audits and reviews;
  ○ Feedback from interested parties;
  ○ Techniques, products, or procedures, which could be used to improve the ISMS performance and effectiveness;
  ○ Status of preventive and corrective actions;
  ○ Feedback from interested parties;
  ○ Results from effectiveness measurements;
  ○ Follow-up actions from previous management reviews;
  ○ Any changes that could affect the ISMS; and
  ○ Recommendations for improvement?

7.3 Review output

❑ Do outputs from management reviews include actions relative to:
  ○ The Information Security Management System (and its processes) improvement
  ○ Product improvement (related to customer requirements)
  ○ Resource needs
  ○ Improvement in the effectiveness of the ISMS.
  ○ Update of the risk assessment and risk management plan?

❑ Are modifications of procedures and controls that affect information security, respond to internal or

external events that may impact of the ISMS, including changes to:
- o Business requirements;
- o Security requirements;
- o Business processes affecting the existing business requirements;
- o Regulatory or legal requirements;
- o Contractual requirements; and
- o Levels of risk and/or criteria for accepting risks?
- o Resource needs.
- o Improvement to how the effectiveness of controls is being measured?

8 ISMS Improvement

8.1 Continual improvement

❑ Does the organization continually improve the effectiveness of the Information Security Management System through the use of:
- o Information security policy and objectives
- o Audit results
- o Analysis of data
- o Corrective and preventive actions
- o Management review?

8.5.2 Corrective Action

❑ Does the organization take action to eliminate the causes of nonconformities?

❑ Does a documented procedure exist to define the requirements for:
- o Reviewing nonconformities (including customer complaints)
- o Determining the causes of nonconformities
- o Evaluating the need for action to ensure that nonconformities do not recur
- o Determining and implementing the action needed
- o Records of the results of the action taken

- Reviewing corrective action taken?

❑ Is the status of corrective actions reviewed during management review?

8.5.3 Preventive action

❑ Does the organization determine action to eliminate the causes of potential nonconformities in order to prevent their occurrence?
❑ Is there a documented procedure to define the requirements for:
- Determining potential nonconformities and their causes
- Evaluating the need for action to prevent occurrence of nonconformities
- Determining and implementing action needed
- Records of results of action taken
- Reviewing preventive action taken?

Chapter Seven: Organizational Security Management

Ten areas in which executives and auditors can quantifiably improve the security posture of any organization

Points to Remember

✓ Adding "Security Management" to your IMS will harden your organization against the threats of today's world while also making it more robust and competitive.

✓ If you are already auditing the security of your organization and its processes to approved sets of standards, or (better yet) International standards like ISO 9000 or ISO 14000, you are half-way there. If you are already auditing to ISO 28000, you ARE there. If the latter is the case, you already know what I am about to tell you.

✓ Organizations need to make security one of their missions, and then approach it like any other: establish **policies and procedures, conduct risk assessments, implement processes, identify** corrective actions, and establish a mindset of continual improvement.

Industrial espionage, hacker/cyber-attacks, natural disasters, disgruntled former employees, HAZMAT spills, and (let's face it) terrorist attacks can close an organization indefinitely, not to mention exacting a concurrent, incidental, toll in personnel or equipment.

Organizations have an ethical as well as an economic imperative to assess and *harden* their security structures. These days, auditors can and should assess the security posture of their organizations as part of the organization's overall auditing strategy. Security Management can also be an indispensable part of an organization's Integrated Management System.

ISO 28000: Supply Chain Security Management can help to ensure the security of any organization. It was developed in response to the transportation and logistics industries' needs for a commonly applicable security management system specific to the supply chain. The elements are applicable to any organization's mission.

The main elements of the ISO 28000 Standard are:

- Security Management Policy
- Security Planning (risk assessment, regulatory requirements, objectives, and targets
- Implementation and Operation (Responsibilities and competence, communication, documentation, operational control, and emergency preparedness)
- Auditing, Corrective and Preventive Action
- Management Review and Continual Improvement.

Organizations already certified to ISO 9000 or ISO 14000 are already well on their way to ISO 28000 certification and to a hardened security posture – the envy of your competitors. These three International Standards mutually support each other, as shown in table 7-1; and security-minded auditors and consultants will work with an organization's existing strategic planning, process management, and documentation, to synergistically increase security, as well as the more traditional challenges, like efficiency, safety, profitability, and regulatory compliance.

Table 7-1 shows how security management fits into, and supports an IMS. You can see that you have already done, or are currently doing, everything you need for an effective IMS.

Table 7-1 Fitting security management into the IMS

IMS

Requirement/Opportunity	ISO 9000	ISO 14000	ISO 27000	ISO 28000	MVO 8000
Standard and explanation	X	X	X	X	X
Top management involvement	X	X	X	X	X
Employee ownership	X	X	X	X	X
Reflected in Strategic Plan	X	X	X	X	X
Process Oriented	X	X	X	X	X
Resistance at first	X	X	X	X	X
Documentation required	X	X	X	X	X
Training	X	X	X	X	X
Manual and checklists for structure	X	X	X	X	X
Capable of self-audit	X	X	X	X	X
Consolidates other compliance requirements in common OP	X	X	X	X	X
Feedback loops established	X	X	X	X	X
Corrective and Preventive action	X	X	X	X	X
Accountability established	X	X	X	X	X

Ten areas in which executives and auditors can quantifiably harden the security of their organizations

The ten areas which follow contain segments of a checklist that I use when I audit or consult in supply chain security management.

1. Organizing for Security Management

> *Things refuse to be mismanaged long – Ralph Waldo Emerson*

Effective security management means that the organization must establish, document, maintain, and continually identify security threats, assess risks, and control/mitigate their consequences. The organization must look at all the functions it performs and assess them according to the amount of vulnerability and the amount of protection required, as shown in the notional matrix. As the arrows suggest, you want to minimize vulnerability and/ or maximize protection.

Figure 7-1 A vulnerability assessment matrix (example)

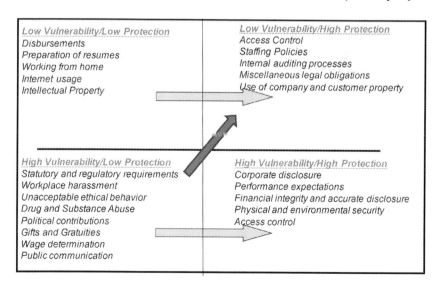

The organization must next define the scope of its Security Management System, including control of outsourced processes that affect the conformity of product or service. That accomplished, the organization must establish (and maintain) an organizational structure of roles, responsibilities, and authorities, consistent with the achievement of the security management policy, objectives, targets, and programs, and these must be defined, documented, and communicated to all responsible individuals.

Top management should provide quantifiable and documented evidence of its commitment to development of the security management system and to improving its effectiveness. Specifically by:

- Appointing a member of top management who, irrespective of other responsibilities is responsible for the design, maintenance, documentation and improvement of the security management system
- Appointing members of management with the necessary authority to ensure that the objectives and targets are implemented
- Identifying and monitoring the expectations of the organization's stakeholders and taking appropriate action to manage these expectations
- Ensuring the availability of adequate resources
- Communicating to the organization the importance of meeting its security management requirements in order to comply with its established policies
- Ensuring any security programs generated from other parts of the organization complement the security management system
- Communicating to the organization the importance of meeting its security management requirements in order to comply with its policy
- Establishing meaningful security metrics and measures of effectiveness
- Ensuring security-related threats, criticalities, and vulnerabilities are evaluated and included in

organizational risk assessments as appropriate (see below)

- Ensuring the viability of the security management objectives, targets, and programs.

2. Security Policies

Top management must develop, as applicable to the mission of the organization, written security policies that are:

- Consistent with the other policies of the organization
- Providing framework for specific security objectives, targets, and programs to be produced
- Consistent with the organization's overall security threat and risk management strategy
- Appropriate to the threats to the organization and the nature and scale of its operations
- Clear in their statement of overall/broad security management objectives
- Compliant with current applicable legislation, regulatory and statutory requirements and with other requirements to which the organization subscribes
- Visibly endorsed by top management
- Documented, implemented, and maintained
- Communicated to all relevant employees and third parties including contractors and visitors with the intent that these persons are made aware of their individual security-related obligations
- Available to stakeholders where appropriate
- Provided for review in case of acquisition or merger, or other change to the business scope, which may affect the relevance of the security management system.

3. Security Risk Assessment

Security Risk Assessment, like any other focused risk assessment, requires the identification and assessment of the *threats, criticalities*, and *vulnerabilities* of the organization and its missions. The organization must establish and maintain a strategy for the ongoing identification, assessment, and mitigation of all its risks, including those related to organizational security. Mitigation means the identification and implementation of effective control measures or courses of action. It is in the execution of the control measures that risk *assessment* becomes risk *management*. We identify notional threats, apply them to different sub-tasks, and assign numerical values in table 7-2.[27]

Table 7-2 Identifying and computing threats

SECURITY TASKS	Terrorist Attack	Utility Loss	Hacker/Cyber Attack	Industrial Espionage	Strike	Agent Spill	Natural Disaster	Falsified reporting	Total	Average
1. Security/Surveillance										
Detecting/identifying unauthorized movement - personnel	9	4	9	9	3	5	8	8	55	7
Detecting/identifying unauthorized movement - vehicles	9	4	9	9	3	5	8	8	55	7
Surveillance of restricted areas	4	4	9	9	3	5	8	8	50	6
Securing incident sites	9	9	9	5	3	5	8	8	56	7
Detection of unauthorized material	9	4	9	5	6	5	8	8	54	7
Surveillance of facility access points	9	4	6	5	6	5	8	8	51	6
Harbor surveillance	6	4	6	5	3	5	8	8	45	6
Automatic security systems	4	4	6	5	3	5	8	8	43	5

Table 7-3 Computing Unadjusted, Adjusted Risk and Risk after applying the COA

Capabilities	Criticality Assessment	Vulnerability Assessment	Threat Assessment	Unadjusted Risk	Environmental Adjustment	Adjusted Risk	Revised Vulnerability	Adj Risk(2) (COA)
1. Security/Surveillance								
Detecting/identifying unauthorized personnel	8	6	4	192	0.5	96	3	48
Detecting/identifying unauthorized vehicles	2	5	2	20	0.4	8	3	5
Surveillance of restricted areas	3	8	4	96	0.2	19	5	12
Securing incident sites	3	6	5	90	0.3	27	4	18
Detection of unauthorized material	4	3	5	60	0.5	30	2	20
Surveillance of facility access points	4	2	6	48	0.2	10	2	17
Harbor surveillance	5	2	2	20	1.2	24	2	24
Automatic security systems	4	3	5	60	0.7	42	2	28

The (hypothetical) table and bar graph describe computing risk assessment according to the following steps:

---

[27] This is the method that I have written about in my book and in professional journals. You may want to do it differently. It's only necessary to be consistent throughout the risk assessment process.

1. **Risk = Threat x Criticality x Vulnerability**
2. **Adjusted Risk = Threat x Criticality x Vulnerability x Environmental Adjustment**
3. **Predicted Risk = Threat x Criticality x Revised Vulnerability x Environmental Adjustment.**

Figure 7-2 reflects successively taking risk mitigations into account.

Figure 7-2 The risk picture

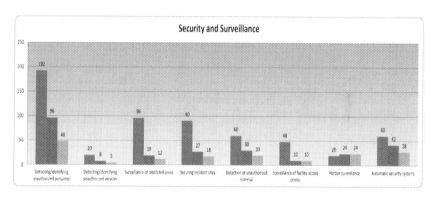

An effective Security Risk Assessment strategy should include identifying (as appropriate):

- Physical failure threats and risks, such as functional failure, incidental damage, malicious damage, or terrorist or criminal action
- Operational threats and risks, including the control of security, human factors, and other activities that affect the organization's performance, condition, or safety
- Environmental or cultural aspects which may either enhance or impair security measures and equipment
- Factors outside of the organization's control such as failures in externally supplied (e.g., outsourced) equipment and services
- Stakeholder threats and risks, such as failure to meet regulatory requirements

- Security equipment, including replacement, maintenance, information and data management, and communications
- Any other threats to the continuity of operations.

4. Security Training and Qualification

The security-minded organization appoints (and entrusts) personnel to operate the Security Management System. Like any other responsible positions in the organization, the people who design, operate, and manage the security equipment and processes must be suitably *qualified* in terms of education, training, certification, and/or experience. Further, these personnel must be fully aware and supportive of:

- The importance of compliance with security management policies and procedures, and to the requirements of the Security Management System as well as their roles in achieving compliance, including emergency preparedness and response
- The potential consequences to the organization's security posture by departing from specified operating procedures.

5. Operational Control

Effective operational control of the Security Management System means that the organization has identified all operations necessary for achieving its stated security management policies, control of all activities, and mitigation of threats identified as posing significant risks. Control also means compliance with legal, statutory, and other regulatory security requirements, the security management objectives, delivery of its security management programs, and the required level of supply chain security (as appropriate).

ISO 28000 Certification requires organizations to ensure that operational control is maintained by:

- Establishing, implementing, and maintaining documented procedures to control situations where their absence could lead to failure to maintain operations
- Establishing and maintaining the requirements for goods or services which impact on security and communicating these to suppliers and contractors.

Where existing designs, installations, operations, etc., are changed, documentation of the changes should address attendant revisions to:

- Organizational structure, roles or responsibilities
- Security management policy, objectives, targets, or programs, processes or procedures.
- Documenting the introduction of new security infrastructure, equipment, or technology, which may include hardware and/or software, should also include the introduction of new contractors or suppliers.

Almost every organization has some kind of security requirements and attendant risks, which, whether upstream or downstream of its activities, can have a profound influence on its operations, products, or services. Identifying, evaluating, and mitigating threats posed from upstream or downstream supply chain activities is as essential as performing the same functions inside your own fence line. The organization requires controls to mitigate potential security impacts to it and to other nodes in the supply chain as well.

6. Communication and Documentation

The organization must have procedures for ensuring that pertinent security management information is communicated to and from relevant employees, contractors, and stakeholders. This applies to outsourced operations as well as those taking place within the organization. This is especially important when dealing with sensitive or classified information.

Additionally, the organization must establish security management system documentation system that includes but is not limited to:

- The Security Management System scope, policy, objectives, and targets
- Description of the main components of the security management system and their interaction, and reference to related documents
- Documents including records determined by the organization to be necessary to ensure the effective planning, operation and control of processes that relate to its significant security threats and risks.

7. Emergency Preparedness and Response

Emergency response may be thought of as conducting normal operations at faster-than-normal speeds, or it may mean something entirely different. The security-minded organization needs to establish, implement, and maintain appropriate plans and procedures (e.g., backing up of records or files) for responses to security incidents and emergency situations, and to prevent and/or mitigate the likely consequences associated with them.

Emergency plans and procedures should include all information dealing with identified facilities or services that may be required during or after incidents or emergency situations, in order to maintain continuity of operations.[28]

Organizations should periodically review the effectiveness of their emergency preparedness, response, and recovery plans and procedures, especially after the occurrence of incidents or emergency situations caused by security breaches and threats. Security-minded managers and auditors will test these procedures periodically (as applicable), including scheduling

---

[28] The best emergency management plans that I have ever seen were for U.S. Naval Bases along the Gulf Coast, where the threat (and likelihood) of hurricanes is perennial and immense.

drills and exercises and developing corrective actions as appropriate.

8. Auditing and Evaluation

Periodic internal or outside security audits determine whether the organization is in compliance with relevant legislation and regulations, industry best practices, and conformance with its own policy and objectives. As with any other audit, organizations need to maintain records of results, findings, and required preventive and corrective action.

Security-minded organizations need to audit their security management plans, procedures, and capabilities. Security audits can include periodic reviews, testing, post-incident reports and lessons learned, performance evaluations, and exercises. Significant findings and observations, once properly evaluated or gamed, should be reflected in revisions or modifications.

9. Preventive and Corrective Action

Auditors discover nonconformities during audits. In doing so, they identify the need for either preventive or corrective action. Top management (hopefully) supports the audit findings and initiates preventive or corrective actions as appropriate.

There is no difference with *security* audits. In fact, the need for corrective action may be even more acute[29].

10. Continual Improvement

Organizational Effectiveness, the basis and underpinning of the ISO International Standards, must be thought of as an ongoing process and not an "end state". It requires top management to

---

[29] ISO 9001:2015 does not use the term "preventive" action. There has always been a subtle difference that no longer needs a separate category.

develop a continuous improvement *mindset* that says that we can always make something better. Continual improvement of organizational security requires top management to review the organization's security management system at planned intervals, in order to ensure its continuing suitability, adequacy, and effectiveness. Security audits and reviews should include assessing opportunities for improvement and the attendant need for changes to the security management system, including security policies and security objectives, plus threats and risks. Organizations already working with ISO 9000 and ISO 14000 can, with minimal effort, expand management reviews to cover security and well as quality and environmental management.

A Security Management Review, either stand-alone or as part of other management reviews (e.g., ISO 9000), should include:

- Evaluations of compliance with legal and regulatory requirements and other requirements to which the organization subscribes
- Communication from external interested parties, including complaints
- The day-to-day security performance of the organization
- Facility or physical plant security (including motion sensors, firewalls, or perimeter fencing)
- The extent to which stated objectives and targets have been met
- The Security Risk Assessment strategy
- Status of corrective and preventive actions, and/or follow-up actions from previous management reviews
- Changing circumstances, including developments in legal and other requirements related to its security aspects
- Recommendations for improvement.
- Outputs from security management reviews should include any decisions and actions changing the Security Management System, together with costs, schedules, and other justifications, and should be consistent with a mindset and commitment to continual improvement.

Summary

Today, more than ever, Security Management is an essential component of a comprehensive integrated management system.

Organizations that cannot conduct their operations in a self-imposed and self-monitored secure environment may cease to exist just as certainly as organizations that cannot maintain operational effectiveness, profitability, or product/service superiority – only faster.

Organizations must *harden* their operations to protect them from either incidental or deliberate attack. Auditors are essential to the hardening process, simply by doing what they do best: auditing.

Chapter Eight: Corporate Responsibility Management – Becoming a Good Company and a Better Neighbor

> **"A man is truly ethical only when he obeys the compulsion to help all life which he is able to assist, and shrinks from injuring anything that lives."**
>
> **Albert Schweitzer 1875-1965**

This chapter discusses adding Corporate Responsibility Management to an Integrated Management System. It also describes MVO 8000, a new international standard in the ISO format that I co-authored and the subject of a book that I wrote several years ago.[30] Both the book and the Standard will help any organization to structure its corporate responsibility management system, and, in doing so, become a better employer and a better neighbor.

More than ever, organizations need to recognize and accept all of the previously unseen responsibilities that involve good citizenship. It is neither easy, nor automatic. For an organization

---

[30] *The Executive's Guide to Corporate Responsibility Management and MVO 8000*

to be a "good citizen", it must succeed across a spectrum of challenges that include (in addition to building a business):

- Community responsibility
- Employee health, safety, and quality of life
- Environmental compliance and a responsible husbanding of limited resources.[31]

In recent years, even the most overconfident CEOs have acknowledged the success of structured management systems like ISO 9000, ISO 14000, and many of the others. In those same recent years, monumental company failures have both underscored the need and created the requirement for CEOs and CFOs to satisfy themselves and attest in writing regarding the veracity of their documentation. Reliance on outsiders, to the exclusion of internal audits and controls, inevitably leads to disaster. Look at ENRON.

MVO 8000 Corporate Responsibility Management Standard

My first book introduced MVO 8000, which I had the privilege to help create. It is not the intention of this Standard to replace the knowledge and skill of the CEO with a cookbook. Rather, MVO 8000 provides CEOs with useful tools to run their organizations as good leaders, managers, and neighbors.

MVO 8000 applies to any organization and can be efficiently integrated into existing management systems. It is derived from statutory and regulatory requirements, internal guidelines, best practices, and (most important) an *ethical imperative* to conduct business honestly and with proper regard for the employee, the customer, and the community. Its input requirements are essentially the same as for any other initiative to be effective, and as specified in international standards that continue to grow in popularity and contribution.

---

[31] "Social" responsibility includes legal, ethical, economic, and philanthropic. That is why I do not use the term in this book. Corporate Responsibility Management is more fitting to our purposes.

Table 8-1 compares the requirements of MVO 8000 with established and proven effective international standards.

Table 8-1 Comparison of general requirements of well-known International Standards with MVO 8000

IMS

Requirement/Opportunity	ISO 9000	ISO 14000	ISO 27000	ISO 28000	MVO 8000
Standard and explanation	X	X	X	X	X
Top management involvement	X	X	X	X	X
Employee ownership	X	X	X	X	X
Reflected in Strategic Plan	X	X	X	X	X
Process Oriented	X	X	X	X	X
Resistance at first	X	X	X	X	X
Documentation required	X	X	X	X	X
Training	X	X	X	X	X
Manual and checklists for structure	X	X	X	X	X
Capable of self-audit	X	X	X	X	X
Consolidates other compliance requirements in common OP	X	X	X	X	X
Feedback loops established	X	X	X	X	X
Corrective and Preventive action	X	X	X	X	X
Accountability established	X	X	X	X	X

MVO 8000 provides a structure for a corporate responsibility management system, and, in doing so, helps organizations to formulate policies and objectives governing company Corporate Responsibility; incorporating statutory and regulatory requirements, and the requirements of company personnel, stakeholders, suppliers, and the community. The Standard itself does not establish any specific ethical standards or values.

MVO 8000 is applicable to every organization planning to:

- Implement, maintain, and improve a corporate responsibility system
- Comply with the established corporate responsibility policies
- Have its corporate responsibility management system certified by an external organization and recognized worldwide
- Confirm by periodic audits that the system is implemented and maintained in accordance with the Standard.

Corporate Responsibility Management Policies

Corporate Responsibility Management policies should not be stand-alone statements. Instead, they must be integral to the mission, operations, and overall strategy of the organization. Policies already developed pursuant to ISO 9000 or ISO 14000 (for example) are definitely appropriate for, and should be included in, the policies developed in accordance with effective corporate responsibility management. CEOs should develop meaningful corporate responsibility management policies as part of their IMS and as a means of establishing standards, and for leading the organizations through mission realization and continual improvement.

Meaningful Corporate Responsibility Management policies should:

- Clearly state management's commitment to high standards of ethical practice,
- Be consistent with management's vision and strategies for the future,
- Include measurable objectives,
- Be widely disseminated within the organization and among outside stakeholders,

- Document its objectives clearly and be reviewed routinely, and
- Be subject to continual improvement.

When determining the corporate responsibility management policies and objectives, management should consider the following:

- The expectations and needs of all interested parties
- Involvement at all levels in the company
- The importance of ethical awareness among all personnel
- The resources necessary to achieve the objectives
- The necessity of continuously improving the Corporate Responsibility Management system
- Communicating the Corporate Responsibility Management policy and objectives within, the organization
- The determination of measurable objectives
- The satisfying of statutory and regulatory requirements.

Code of Ethics and Standards of Conduct

Organizations cannot expect compliance with a Corporate Responsibility Management system if the governing principles of that system are not fully stated and understood by all assigned personnel. Moreover, the procedure by which the principles are imparted on the personnel must include a structured procedure in which personnel receive instruction and signify in writing their understanding of that instruction and their willingness to comply.

Toward that end, organizations should develop comprehensive, documented, codes of ethics and standards of conduct. Personnel should be trained, initially and periodically, on the code of ethics and standards of conduct, and sign an appropriate record affirming their understanding and compliance.

Table 8-2 contains the Code of Ethics and Standards of Conduct clause from MVO 8000. How many of these do your programs already address?

Table 8-2 MVO 8000 Code of Ethics and Standards of Conduct Clause

3.3 Code of Ethics and Standards of Conduct (MVO 8000)

Management will create a Code of Ethics and Standards of Conduct, to include (as applicable):

a) The Corporate Responsibility System

b) Statutory and regulatory requirements

c) Financial integrity and accurate disclosure

d) Formal standards of performance and expectations

e) Harassment

f) Staffing policies

g) The organization's approach to personnel customers, competitors, suppliers, and community

h) Unacceptable ethical behavior as it applies to the organization

i) Legal obligations of the organization and its members

j) Intellectual property

k) Physical and environmental security

l) Access control

m) Proper recording or and disbursement of funds or other assets

n) Use of company and customer property

o) Internet usage

p) Drug and substance abuse policy

q) Public communication

r) Working from home,

s) Internal auditing processes

t) Political contributions

u) Preparation of resumes

v) Wage determinations and gifts and gratuities.

Ethics Awareness Training

For purposes of this Standard, we define ethics awareness training as *"customized training dealing with ethical, safe, and desirable practices in the organization, and how those practices impact on organizational performance and morale".* An effective ethics awareness training program can reduce undesirable or inappropriate behavior.

Management should ensure that its ethics awareness training program includes the following objectives:

- Building awareness of ethical standards and values of individuals and communities;
- Formulating/maintaining a Corporate Responsibility policy and (measurable) objectives;
- Developing and documenting of a code of ethics and standards of conduct; development and implementation of a Corporate Responsibility management system;
- Responsible Business Practices; and
- Communication and interactive skills.

Preparing for Corporate Responsibility Management

Figure 8-1 provides an overview of the Corporate Responsibility Management System establishment and installation process. We have discussed the main points. Now, note the input and output arrows and the feedback.

Figure 8-1 Establishing a Corporate Responsibility Management System

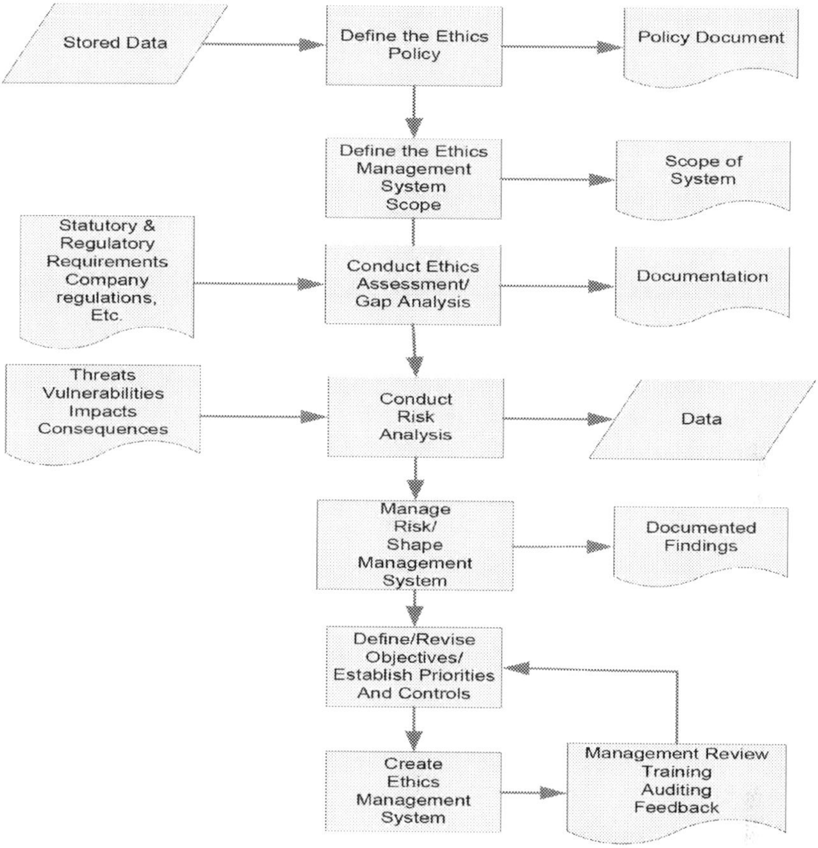

Like the ISO systems, corporate responsibility management in general and MVO 8000 in particular stress continual improvement. Systems and processes should be subject to structured review and every process can always be made better.

Putting Policies and Practices to the Test

Please look at figure 8-2. You might want to devise a way to collect findings like these in your own organization, if you're not doing it already.

*Figure 8-2 Does Management practice ethical conduct?
(as seen by employees)*[32]

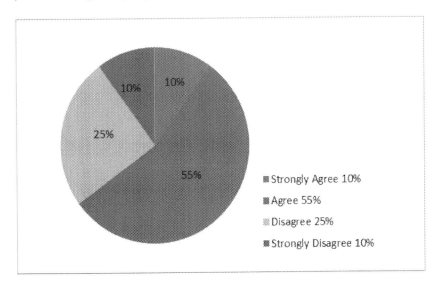

Suppose for a minute that 35% of your employees believed that you and your top management do not act ethically. Think about what you would do. Here are some thoughts:

- You could probably justify your actions and/or take either side of an argument, with almost the same justification; but it's in <u>analyzing</u> both sides that Management gets the right answer
- When the terms used are not specific enough (e.g., "risk"), the survey loses validity
- Surveys will usually present Management with one or more of the following:
    1. Invalid data (too much, too little, too old)
    2. Invalid models or algorithms (Non-specific, outdated, too complicated)
    3. An ethical dilemma, which may not have been immediately apparent

---

[32] Figures are for demonstration only – they are not based on the findings of any actual study.

4. A short – term or personal gain, regardless of the long term effect

Ethics problems (like production problems) should be:

1. Caught sooner/earlier,
2. Properly reported and documented,
3. Investigated/analyzed
4. Action taken as appropriate, including feedback and follow-up

Uncovering an actual wrong-doing must result in something positive for the organization. In the long term, Management must deal with customers and suppliers in an ethical and moral manner or go out of business.

Nobody gets away with anything for long.

Summary

Organizations need a structured corporate responsibility management system like MVO 8000, and here's why.

A. General

- Better risk and crisis identification and management
- Better relations with stakeholders and interested communities
- Increased worker commitment
- Increased productivity potential
- Reduced operating costs
- Enhanced brand value and reputation
- Long - term sustainability for company and society.

B. Specific - Internal Benefits

- A comprehensive Ethics Management System
- A Code of Ethics and Standards of Conduct
- Prevention of ethics, safety, or environmental violations
- The ability to self-audit

Specific - External Benefits

- Certification to an established standard by an international registrar
- Recognition and image enhancement
- A unique and unequalled marketing tool – ahead of its time
- Measurably improved customer and community relations.

Chapter Nine: Facilities Hardening and Contingency Planning

Organizations need to make security one of their key missions, and then approach it like any other: establish policies and procedures, identify threats, conduct risk assessments, implement processes, identify corrective actions, and establish a mindset of continuous improvement. And audit.

This chapter highlights specific topics, in the hope that they will inspire managers to create and maintain robust organizational security programs and operate them as any other indispensable business function. It also amplifies checklists that I use when I audit or consult, available to you (ready to go) at no charge at my website: *www.corprespmgmt.com*. There is much more in my books: *Fixes That Last – The Executive's Guide to Fix It or Lose It Management (2nd Ed), The Executive's Guide To Internal Auditing,* and *Hardening by Auditing.*

Points to Remember

✓ Security-minded organizations need to establish, implement, and maintain appropriate plans and procedures (e.g., backing up of records or files) for responses to security incidents and emergency situations, and to prevent and/or mitigate the likely consequences associated with them.

✓ Emergency response may be thought of as conducting normal business operations at faster-than-normal speeds. It follows, therefore, that normal operations must be compatible (if not identical in many respects) with emergency operations.

✓ Emergency response plans and procedures should include all information dealing with identified facilities or services that may be required during or after incidents, disruptions, or emergency situations, in order to restore continuity of operations.

✓ Organizations should periodically review the effectiveness of their emergency preparedness, response, and recovery plans and procedures, especially after the occurrence of incidents or emergency situations caused by security breaches and/or threats.

✓ Security-minded managers and auditors will test these procedures periodically (as applicable), including scheduling drills and exercises and developing lessons learned and corrective actions as appropriate.

1. What is Contingency Planning and where does it fit?

Here is a practical definition for Contingency Planning from an excellent book: *"The process of planning for response to an event or emergency, managing the escalation of an emergency into a crisis condition, recovery and resumption of activities from an emergency or crisis for the infrastructure, critical processes, and other elements of a business or organization. The process of building all the elements of a plan focused on mitigating any interruption to business operations."*[33]

---

[33] Halibozek, E. et al, *The Corporate Security Professional's Handbook on Terrorism, Butterworth-Heinemann, Burlington, MA, 2008*

As figure 9-1 implies, thorough contingency planning requires:

- The identification of every aspect and requirement of the organization – all missions and under both normal and emergency operations;
- Continuous feedback between the planning and execution of those normal and emergency operations;
- The establishment of goals, objectives, metrics, and measures of effectiveness (MOE) with which to assess the feedback, and identify/analyze gaps between the actual and the required;
- Systems of controls for processing the results of the gap identification and analyses; and
- A Continuous Improvement *imperative* and mindset to motivate and optimize the entire process.

Figure 9-1 Contingency Planning Content

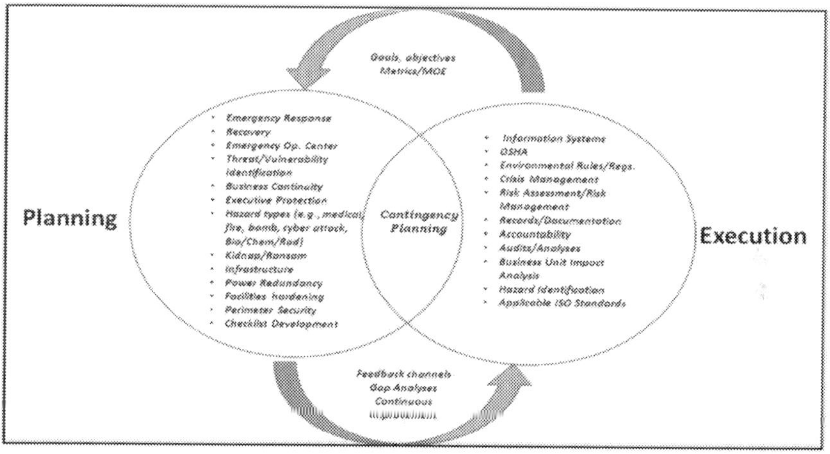

You might think that contingency planning strongly resembles regular organizational planning. You would be right.

2. To Plan or not to Plan – There is no Question

Many of us, in our auditing adventures, have met managers who consider contingency planning unnecessary. Their reasons vary, but when they directly or indirectly discourage contingency planning they deny their organizations an *adhesive* that more fully bonds their people and processes together, through the identification and protection of all products and services, risks and rewards, lines of authority, responsibility, and feedback. When you pla for contingencies:

- An incident management capability is enabled for effective response
- Critical activities are identified
- Acceptable (and unacceptable) levels of risk are identified as a function of threat and impact analysis
- Information flows are enabled, reinforced, or terminated as a function of
  - Confidentiality
  - Integrity
  - Availability
  - Currency
  - Expedience
- The interaction of the organization with regulators, communities, governments, and (possibly) host nations is developed, documented, and understood
- Personnel are trained to respond quickly, meaningfully, and *safely* to incidents or disruptions – natural or man-made
- Key lines of authority, communication, and supply/ resupply are reinforced and secured
- Resources are identified, prioritized, and programmed
- Regulatory compliance responsibilities are understood
- Stakeholders understand their duties in direct or indirect support of the organization
- The organization's reputation is protected and (most likely) enhanced.

3. Contingency Planning and Contingency Plans – Not the same

Much has been written about the difference between the process of "planning" and the creation of "plans." Some of our greatest Military thinkers have praised the process of planning and condemned the creation of arsenals of "plans".[34]

Even the most thoughtfully developed plans often fall short in their implementation because they either:

- Never get fully disseminated; or
- Cannot be executed by on-scene management; or
- Leave out critical considerations; or
- Require injections of specialized training; or
- Never get exercised, and (accordingly) never get adjusted; or
- Never get updated to reflect new procedures or capital improvements; or
- Were plagiarized from a similar but separate organization.

The list could go on, but you get the idea.

If a required course of action is contained within a current plan (i.e., it was anticipated), the current plan survives intact. However, if the required course of action is (in some manner) beyond the current plan, re-planning is necessary, which wastes time and manpower and degrades mission effectiveness.

All plans need to have built-in "tripwires" or "pre-planned responses," that allow on-scene managers to execute when they are satisfied that pre-determined criteria have been met. Timeliness of execution should be incorporated into the strategy and structure of any plan. However, if the decision to execute requires the staffing, concurrence, and/or permission of higher authority, that timeliness can be diminished or even lost completely.

The Military helped solve the problem of too many plans and not enough planning, and of "execution by committee" with the concept of Situational Awareness, or the ability to recognize a situation (or a change in a situation) identify and assess

---

[34] Patton and Eisenhower were two – nice to know that they agreed on something.

the options, select a course of action, AND translate it into *actionable* orders. For the rest of us, civilian organizations maintain situational awareness when they share, internally and externally, the same operational (big) picture; and deviations or fluctuations are recognized more rapidly by managers, who can implement corrective actions almost spontaneously. Managers and auditors should look for and encourage situational awareness when they look at the *feedback, communication, and continuous improvement* mechanisms in the organization.

Other, more specific opportunities for Management to incorporate situational awareness can be found in:

- Standard operating procedures or SOPs
- Information management (including weather prediction)
- Report generation and simplification
- Pre-planned responses
- Alarm and alert systems
- Training and qualification systems
- Executive "dashboards."
- Clear-cut lines of authority (everybody knows who's in charge; and local managers have sufficient authority to initiate and support expedient recovery).

Top Management needs to focus on this last bullet. The ability of an on-scene manager to enter into contracts or to purchase needed goods and services unilaterally is, in my experience, absolutely essential during contingency operations.

Several years ago, while working as a Military analyst, I helped to reconstruct contingency response command and control at major U.S. Navy shore installations on the Gulf Coast before, during, and after hurricanes Katrina, Rita, and Wilma. The analysis confirmed (to nobody's surprise) the following with regard to contingency planning and situational awareness:

1. *Installation commanders and staffs had prepared documented contingency plans and situational awareness strategies from which to execute flexible responses. Once vital services were restored on-base, the Military went into the local communities to help. Local governments and FEMA lacked the required preparation, training, and expertise. Picture the movie: "In The Heat of the Night", with a dysfunctional town council and a mayor who sold tractors.*

2. *Those same installation commanders had conducted exercises, gathered feedback and "lessons learned" and honed their future responses long before onset of those hurricanes. Local governments and FEMA had not.*

3. *Local governments turned to the Military not only to restore utilities (e.g., providing emergency power to local hospitals and cell phone towers) but to set up command centers in the cities and "assist" local officials through recovery and restoration.*

4. *FEMA routinely usurped power and took over direction of local emergency operations. FEMA should never have tried, for example, to tell Naval air station commanders how to conduct flight operations or tell (U.S. Coast Guard) port captains how to conduct search and rescue operations.*

Figure 9-2 describes the Contingency Plan "continuum. That is, the path from and back to normal operations after a disruptive incident. The path takes the organization through Response, Continuity, Recovery/Resumption, and back to Normal. The ability of the organization to travel safely and expeditiously along this path depends on the suitability and robustness of the planning, the consistency and likeness of normal and contingency operations, and the ability of on-scene personnel to react without the need for further guidance and direction from above.

Figure 9-2 The Contingency Plan Continuum

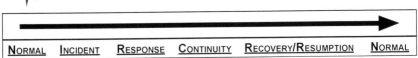

| NORMAL | INCIDENT | RESPONSE | CONTINUITY | RECOVERY/RESUMPTION | NORMAL |

Contingency planning, according to *NFPA 1600* consists of five components:

1. The Strategic Plan
2. The Emergency Operations/Response Plan
3. The Mitigation Plan
4. The Recovery Plan
5. The Continuity Plan.

However, the possible establishment of five separate plans (possibly created by five separate levels or functions) creates numerous real and potential interoperability complications, especially over time, as some activities change and others do not. The "Strategic Plan" required is actually a subset of the overall strategic plan governing the organization. With that in mind, a more streamlined contingency planning strategy (see figure 9-3) would likely be more executable.

Figure 9-3 Evolving the Contingency Plan

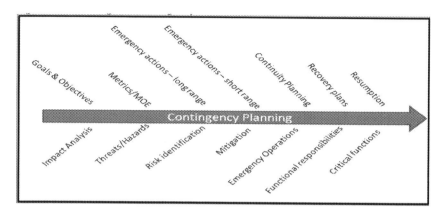

All the components of the diagram must be combined, revised, and combined again to create operating plans for normal operations anyway. The shift to a contingency scenario should be as automatic and transparent as possible.

3. Executing Contingency Planning (aka Emergency Response)

As discussed, organizations must be capable of *executing* contingency plans – quickly, efficiently, and completely, and contingency operations should be *as close as possible to normal operations*, especially since the goal of contingency operations is the rapid restoration of normal operations. Accordingly, contingency operations should support normal operations and (just like normal operations) should reflect the following:

- Total asset visibility throughout the supply chain
- Organic self-auditing and data collection and analysis
- Process mapping and balancing
- Restoration goals (e.g., pieces/hour after 24 hours)
- Clearly defined lines of authority and responsibility
- Up-to-date threat, vulnerability, needs, and risk assessments
- Personnel qualifications, based on needs assessments
- Acquisition authority of on-site management.

- Exercises that generate lessons learned and feedback.

Exercises should include the involvement and participation of local authorities, or they will risk communications and interoperability problems when the real thing happens. The involvement of the local authorities of host nations (when doing business outside the U.S.) is even more important. By way of example, commercial ships entering foreign or domestic ports are required to have "port security plans" that mesh with the security plans of the ports, in order that the actions of both ship and port support and complement each other. Responses are automatic and unilateral and each player knows what to expect from the other.

Organizations can both enhance and expedite their preparations for exercise or actual contingencies by conducting informal "table top" exercises, during which representatives from involved organizations come together to "game" potential contingencies. They develop cooperative reactions to imposed threat scenarios. Table top exercises can be quick, inexpensive, vehicles to identify and assess threats, develop needs and risk assessments, and prioritize allocation of personnel and funding. The results of a structured table top exercise can become very meaningful and "action-able" audit findings.

4. Continuity and Recovery – Back to (a "New") Normal as Quickly as Possible

Auditors witness (and often pass judgment on) the exercise of authority, responsibility, and accountability by Top Management. We audit quality, environmental compliance, supply chain security, and the like. We look at sales, profit and loss, and training – all in the context of *how* the organization should operate. Accordingly, we can lose sight of the fact that Top Management has (as its most fundamental duty) the responsibility for maintaining the ability of the organization *to operate,* and to operate without disruption. That is, the ability to maintain "continuity".

British Standard 25999 defines *business continuity* as "the strategic and tactical capability of the organization to plan for and respond to incidents and business disruptions in order to continue business operations at an acceptable pre-defined level;" and *business continuity management* as "a holistic management process that identifies potential threats to an organization and the impacts to business operations that those threats, if realized, might cause, and which provides a framework for building organizational resilience with the capability for an effective response that safeguards the interests of its key stakeholders, reputation, brand, and value creating activities."

Recoveries are measured not in terms of days or hours, but rather in terms of re-establishments or re-achievements of previously defined objectives. For example:

- The resumption of product or service delivery after an incident; or
- The resumption of performance of an activity or service after an incident; or
- The recovery of an IT system or software after an incident.

Again, there must be genuine commonality and cohesion of structure, processes, and lines of authority for an organization to move from normal to emergency, contingency, continuity, to recovery and (back) to normal operations. However, Management should have as its recovery goal, the establishment of a "new" normal. That is, come back from the contingency stronger or better.

Summary

All organizations are subject to incidents and disruptions of operations. Disruptions can be the result of terrorist or cyber-attack, natural disasters such as hurricanes, earthquakes, or floods, or internal occurrences such as fires, utility outages, hacking, or HAZMAT spills. Managers and auditors must develop and refine the ability of organizations to react to the emergency, mitigate it, and initiate restorations until normal operations are fully resumed – all while protecting the welfare and safety of their personnel and the community.

Contingency planning and all that goes with it should be considered not as a cosmetic or mandated expenditure of time and funding, but as an extension of normal management processes – one that adds great value to the organization. Good managers can do it – good auditors can help.

APPENDIX ONE

ORGANIZATIONAL SECURITY MANAGEMENT CHECKLIST

ITEM 4.1 GENRAL REQUIREMENTS

Has the organization established, documented, maintained, and continually improved an effective security management system for identifying security threats, assessing risks, and controlling/mitigating their consequences?

Has the organization defined the scope of its security management system, including control of outsourced processes that affect the conformity with these requirements?

ITEM: 4.2 SECURITY MANAGEMENT POLICY

Has top management developed a written security policy, and is it:

a) Consistent with other organizational policies
b) Providing framework for specific security objectives, targets, and programs to be produced
c) Consistent with the organization's overall security threat and risk management framework
d) Appropriate to the threats to the organization and the nature and scale of its operations
e) Clear in its statement of overall/broad security management objectives

f) Committed to compliance with current applicable legislation, regulatory and statutory requirements and with other requirements to which the organization subscribes

g) Visibly endorsed by top management

h) Documented, implemented, and maintained

i) Communicated to all relevant employees and third parties including contractors and visitors with the intent that these persons are made aware of their individual security-related obligations

j) Available to stakeholders where appropriate

k) Provided for review in case of acquisition or merger, or other change to the business scope, which may affect the relevance of the security management system?

ITEM 4.3: SECURITY RISK ASSESSMENT PLANNING

❑ Has the organization established and maintained procedures for ongoing identification and assessment of security threats and security management-related threats and risks, and the identification and implementation of necessary management control measures?

❑ Are threats and risk identification, assessment, and control methods appropriate to the nature and scale of the operations?

❑ Does the risk assessment include:

a) Physical failure threats and risks, such as functional failure, incidental damage, malicious damage or terrorist or criminal action

b) Operational threats and risks, including the control of security, human factors, and other activities that affect the organization's performance, condition, or safety

c) Natural environmental events which may render security measures and equipment ineffective

d) Factors outside of the organization's control such as failures in externally supplied equipment and services

e) Stakeholder threats and risks, such as failure to meet regulatory requirements or damaged reputation
f) Design and installation of security equipment including replacement, maintenance, etc.
g) Information and data management and communications
h) A threat to the continuity of operations?

☐ Are the results of these assessments considered and do they provide input into:

a) Security management objectives and targets
b) Security management programs
c) The determination of requirements for the design, specification, and installation
d) Identification of adequate resources including staffing levels
e) Identification of training needs and skills
f) Development of operational controls
g) The organization's overall threat and risk management framework?

☐ Is the organization's methodology for risk identification and assessment:

a. Defined with respect to its scope, nature, and timing, to ensure that it is proactive rather than reactive
b. Include a collection of information related to security threats and risks
c. Provide for the classification of threats and risks and identification of those that are to be avoided, eliminated, or controlled
d. Provide for the monitoring of actions to ensure effectiveness and the timeliness of their implementation?

❑ Has the organization established, implemented, and maintained a procedure:

- a) To identify and have access to the applicable legal requirements and other requirements to which the organization subscribes related to its security threat and risks
- b) To determine how these requirements apply to its security threats and risks?

❑ Does the organization have documented security management objectives, and do they take into account:

- a) Legal, statutory, and other security regulatory requirements
- b) Security-related threats and risks
- c) Technological and other options
- d) Financial, operational, and business requirements
- e) Views of appropriate stakeholders?

❑ Are the security objectives:

- a) Consistent with the organization's commitment to continual improvement
- b) Quantified (where practicable)
- c) Communicated to all relevant employees and third parties, including contractors, with the intent that these persons are made aware of their personal obligations
- d) Reviewed periodically to ensure that they remain relevant and consistent with the security management policy. Where necessary the security management objectives shall be amended accordingly.

❑ Are security management targets established, implemented, and maintained, and are they:

- a) To an appropriate level of detail

b) Specific, measurable, achievable, relevant and time-based (where practicable)
c) Communicated to all relevant employees and third parties including contractors with the intent that these persons are made aware of their individual obligations
d) Reviewed periodically to ensure that they remain relevant and consistent wit the security management objectives, and amended accordingly?

❑ Are there security management programs established for achieving the organization's objectives and targets, and are they optimized and prioritized, and do they describe:

a) Designated authority and responsibility for achieving objectives and targets
b) The means and time scale by which the objectives and targets will be achieved, and are they reviewed/ amended periodically to ensure that they remain effective?

ITEM 4.4: IMPLEMENTATION & OPERATION

4.4.1 Structure, authority, and responsibility for security management

❑ Has the organization established and maintained an organizational structure of roles, responsibilities, and authorities, consistent with the achievement of its security management policy, objectives, targets, and programs, and are these defined, documented, and communicated to responsible individuals?
❑ Does top management provide evidence of its commitment to development of the security management system and improving its effectiveness by:

a) Appointing a member of top management who, irrespective of other responsibilities is responsible for the design, maintenance, documentation and improvement of the security management system

b) Appointing members of management with the necessary authority to ensure that the objectives and targets are implemented

c) Identifying and monitoring the requirements and expectations of the organization's stakeholders and taking appropriate action to manage these expectations

d) Ensuring the availability of adequate resources

e) Communicating to the organization the importance of meeting its security management requirements in order to comply with its policy

f) Ensuring any security programs generated from other parts of the organization complement the security management system

g) Communicating to the organization the importance of meeting its security management requirements in order to comply with its policy

h) Ensuring security-related threats and risks are evaluated and included in organizational threat and risk assessments as appropriate

i) Ensuring the viability of the security management objectives, targets, and programs?

4.4.2 Competence, training, and awareness

❑ Does the organization ensure that personnel responsible for the design, operation, and management of security equipment and processes are suitably qualified in terms of education, training and/or experience, and has the organization established and maintained procedures for making persons working for it or on its behalf aware of:

a) The importance of compliance with the security management policy and procedures, and to the requirements of the security management system

b) Their roles and responsibilities in achieving compliance with the security management policy and procedures and with the requirements of the security management system, including emergency preparedness and response requirements

c) The potential consequences to the organization's security by departing from specified operating procedures?

4.3 Communication

❑ Does the organization have procedures for ensuring that pertinent security management information is communicated to and from relevant employees, contractors, and stakeholders?

❑ Is proper consideration given to the sensitivity of security-related information?

4.4.4 Documentation

❑ Has the organization established a security management documentation system that includes but is not limited to the following:

a) The security policy, objectives, and targets
b) Description of the security management system scope
c) Description of the main elements of the security management system and their interaction, and reference to related documents
d) Documents, including records, required by this International Standard
e) Documents including records determined by the organization to be necessary to ensure the effective planning, operation and control of processes that relate to its significant security threats and risks

4.5 Document and data control

❑ Has the organization established and maintained procedures for controlling all documents, data, and information required by Clause 4 of this International Standard to ensure that:

a) These documents, data and information can be located and accessed only by authorized individuals
b) These documents, data, and information are periodically reviewed, revised as necessary, and approved for adequacy by authorized personnel
c) Current versions of relevant documents, data, and information are available at all locations where operations essential to the effective functioning of the security management system are performed
d) Obsolete documents, data, and information are promptly removed from all points of issue and points of use, or otherwise assured against unintended use
e) Archival documents, data, and information retained for legal or knowledge preservation purposes or both are suitably identified
f) These documents, data, and information are secure, and if in electronic form are adequately backed up and can be recovered?

4.6 Operational control

❏ Has the organization identified operations that are necessary for achieving:

a) Its security management policy
b) The control of activities and mitigation of threats identified as having significant risk
c) Compliance with legal, statutory and other regulatory security requirements
d) The security management objectives
e) The delivery of its security management programs
f) The required level of supply chain security

❏ Has the organization ensured that these operations and activities are carried out under specified conditions by:

a) Establishing, implementing, and maintaining documented procedures to control situations where their absence could lead to failure to achieve the operations and activities listed above
b) Evaluating any threats posed from upstream supply chain activities and applying controls to mitigate these impacts to the organization and other downstream supply chain operators
c) Establishing and maintaining the requirements for goods or services which impact on security and communicating these to suppliers and contractors?

❑ Where existing designs, installations, operations, etc., are revised, do the revisions include:

a) Revised organizational structure, roles or responsibilities
b) Revised security management policy, objectives, targets, or programs
c) Revised processes or procedures
d) The introduction of new infrastructure, security equipment or technology, which may include hardware and/or software
e) The introduction of new contractors, suppliers or personnel, as appropriate?

4.7 Emergency preparedness, response and security recovery

❑ Has the organization established, implemented, and maintained appropriate plans and procedures to identify the potential for and responses to, security incidents and emergency situations, and for preventing and mitigating the likely consequences associated with them?
❑ Do the plans and procedures include information on the provision of maintenance of any identified, facilities or services that can be required during or after incidents or emergency situations?

❑ Does the organization periodically review the effectiveness of its emergency preparedness, response and security recovery plans and procedures, in particular after the occurrence of incidents or emergency situations caused by security breaches and threats, and are these procedures periodically tested (as applicable)?

4.8: CHECKING AND CORRECTIVE ACTION

4.8.1 Security performance measurement and monitoring

❑ Has the organization established and maintained procedures to monitor and measure the performance of its security management system, and does it consider associated threats, risks, including potential deterioration of mechanisms and their consequences, and do these procedures provide for:

❑ Both qualitative and quantitative measurements, appropriate to the needs of the organization

❑ Monitoring the extent to which the organization's security management policy, objectives, and targets are met

❑ Proactive measures of performance that monitor compliance with the security management programs, operational control criteria and applicable legislation, statutory and other security regulatory requirements

❑ Reactive measures of performance to monitor security-related deteriorations, failures, incidents, non-conformances and other historical evidence of deficient security management system performance

❑ Recording data and results of monitoring and measurement sufficient to facilitate subsequent corrective and preventive action analysis, and if monitoring equipment is needed are there maintenance and calibration procedures, and are records of calibration kept?

4.8.2 System evaluation

❑ Does the organization evaluate security management plans, procedures, and capabilities through periodic reviews, testing, post-incident reports, lessons learned, performance evaluations, and exercises, and are significant changes in these factors reflected immediately in the procedures?

❑ Does the organization periodically evaluate compliance with relevant legislation and regulations, industry best practices, and conformance with its own policy and objectives?

❑ Are records kept of the results of these periodic evaluations?

4.8.3 Security-related failures, incidents, non-conformance and corrective and preventive actions

❑ Has the organization established, implemented, and maintained procedures for defining responsibility and authority for:

    a) Evaluating and initiating preventive actions to identify potential failures of security in order that they may be prevented from occurring

    b) The investigation of security-related failures, including near misses and false alarms

    c) Incidents and emergency situations

    d) Non-conformances

    e) Taking action to mitigate any consequences arising from such failures, incidents, and non-conformances

    f) The initiation and completion of corrective actions

    g) The confirmation of the effectiveness of corrective actions taken?

❑ Are all proposed corrective and preventive actions reviewed through the security threat and risk assessment process prior to implementation?

❏ Are corrective and preventive actions taken appropriate for the magnitude of the problems and commensurate with the security management-related risks and threats likely to be encountered?

4.8.4 Control of records

❏ Has the organization established and maintained records as necessary to demonstrate conformity to the requirements of its security management system and of this International Standard, and the results achieved?
❏ Has the organization established, implemented, and maintained procedures for the identification, storage, protection, retrieval, retention, and disposal of records?
❏ Are the records legible, identifiable, and traceable?
❏ Are electronic and digital documentation rendered tamper-proof, securely backed-up, and accessible only by authorized personnel?

4.8.5 Audit

Has the organization established, implemented, and maintained a security management audit program and does it ensure that audits of the security management system are carried out at planned intervals, in order to determine whether or not the security management system:

a) Conforms to planned arrangements for security management including the requirements of the whole of Clause 4 of this specification
b) Has been properly implemented and maintained
c) Is effective in meeting the organization's security management policies and objectives

❏ Review the results of previous audits and the actions taken to rectify non-conformances
❏ Provide information on the results of audits to management

❑ Verify that the security equipment and personnel are appropriately deployed?

❑ Is the audit schedule based on the results of threat and risk assessments of the organization's activities, and the results of previous audits, and do the audit procedures cover the scope frequency, methodologies, and competencies, as well as the responsibilities and requirements for conducting audits and reporting results, and are audits, where possible, conducted by personnel independent of those having direct responsibility for the activity being examined?

ITEM 5: MANAGEMENT REVIEW AND CONTINUAL IMPROVEMENT

❑ Does top management review the organization's security management system at planned intervals, to ensure its continuing suitability, adequacy, and effectiveness, and do reviews include assessing opportunities for improvement and the need for changes to the security management system, including security policy and security objectives and threats and risks. Records of the management reviews shall be retained.

❑ Do inputs to management reviews include:

a) Results of audits and evaluations of compliance with legal requirements and with other requirements to which the organization subscribes
b) Communication from external interested parties, including complaints
c) The security performance of the organization
d) The extent to which objectives and targets have been met
e) Status of corrective and preventive actions
f) Follow-up actions from previous management reviews
g) Changing circumstances, including developments in legal and other requirements related to its security aspects
h) Recommendations for improvement?

Do outputs from management reviews include any decisions and actions related to possible changes to security policy, objectives, targets, and other elements of the security management system, consistent with the commitment to continual improvement?

APPENDIX TWO

SAMPLE OPERATING PROCEDURE (OP) FOR CORPORATE RESPONSIBILITY MANAGEMENT (Ref: MVO 8000)

INTEGRATED MANAGEMENT SYSTEM CORPORATE RESPONSIBILITY MANAGEMENT	
Operational Procedure: OP XX – 0X Revision: A	
Prepared by & Date	
Approved by & Date	Vice President, Human Resource Management
Approved by & Date	President

1. PURPOSE AND SCOPE

XXX's Corporate Responsibility Management System (now included in Volume I) reflects the ethical roles and responsibilities of all our operations, customer relations, and impacts on the community, as well as our commitment to all statutory and regulatory requirements. The requirements of the **MVO 8000 Corporate Responsibility Management Standard** that are not applicable to our business are excluded from the scope of the Corporate Responsibility Management System.

Unethical behavior is never justified. Toward that end, all XXX personnel must understand that:

a) Stretching ethical boundaries leads to unethical behavior
b) Unethical acts are unethical, whether or not they are discovered
c) Unethical acts are never in the best interests of the Organization
d) XXX is held responsible for the conduct of all its personnel.

2. BACKGROUND AND PROCEDURE

2.1 PROCEDURE

2.1.1 Management Decision Making and accountability

XXX's reputation depends upon all of the decisions we make and the actions we take daily, and our *values* define how we make and evaluate our decisions and actions.

XXX is an organization of decision makers. Decisions made at all levels in XXX will satisfy the following conditions. Decision makers will:

a) Know that a decision must be made.
b) Know that decisions must be made within specific periods of time.
c) Confront a small number of well-defined options.
d) Know what is needed to make good decision.
e) Accept responsibility for their decisions.

XXX decision makers must consider the impact of their actions on the entire organization. Moreover, other personnel involved in the decision (perhaps with only fragmentary knowledge of a particular organizational process), must be alert for irresponsible or unethical practices and take appropriate action when discovered. Decision makers will take *informed* risks that enable XXX to create new business opportunities and to challenge existing business practices.

2.1.2 Involvement of Management

Management will demonstrate its ethical involvement and oversight of customers, suppliers, company personnel, external board members (as applicable), other stakeholders, and the community by:

Communicating to all levels the importance of satisfying the requirements, standards, and values used by XXX to carry out its business,

Communicating to all levels the importance of satisfying statutory and regulatory requirements in the practice of company ethics,

a) Implementing the company's ethics policies and objectives,
b) Carrying out a program of internal audits.

2.1.3 Corporate Responsibility Management Policy

Management will determine a policy and ensure that the policy formulated:

a) Is suitable and contiguous with the needs of XXX,
b) Is consistent with statutory and regulatory requirements,
c) Provides for continuous improvement of the Corporate Responsibility Management System.

Management will periodically review the effectiveness of the Corporate Responsibility Management System and determine whether or not:

a) The System should be modified,
b) Policies have to be modified, or objectives amended,
c) There is a need for corrective and preventive action.

XXX will train all personnel on the Corporate Responsibility Management System, its importance to our ethical operation, and how it applies to their positions and functions. XXX will establish requirements with regard to the training, qualification, and instruction of all personnel and, in addition, will set standards for competence, experience, and training in the following areas related to the Corporate Responsibility Management System:

a) Occupational Safety and Health,
b) Energy conservation
c) Hazardous Material Control and Management
d) Pollution prevention
e) Recycling
f) Contracting
g) Procurement
h) Internal auditing
i) Finance and accounting.

Management will develop and schedule Corporate Responsibility awareness training for all personnel, and record and evaluate all training activities related to the Corporate Responsibility Management System. All personnel will receive 10 hours of Ethics and Corporate Responsibility Management training per year.

The VP, HRM will establish an "Ethics Hotline" for the reporting of unethical conduct by XXX employees or sub-contractors.

2.1.4 Complaints Procedure

Management will provide employees with a process for communicating instances of unacceptable behavior, to include:

a) The complaint submission procedure
b) Responsibilities for complaints procedure administration,
c) Confidentiality of complaints,
d) Appeal rights of personnel accused.

2.1.5 Personnel Representation

Management will create a committee within XXX:

1) To monitor the ethical functioning of XXX

2) To define objectives, tasks, responsibilities, authorities, and procedures in the operation of the Corporate Responsibility System
3) To review instances of reported violations
4) To administer XXX's sanctions.

2.1.6 Sanctions

In order to manage, mitigate, or prevent unacceptable ethical behavior, XXX will develop a system of sanctions to include:

a) Definition and description undesirable ethical behavior in XXX,
b) The manner in which unacceptable ethical conduct is reported,
c) The manner in which corrective action will be taken, and
d) The manner in which personal information is documented and recorded.

2.1.7 Code of Ethics and Standards of Conduct

Management will create a Code of Ethics and Standards of Conduct, to include (as applicable):

a) The Corporate Responsibility Management System
b) Statutory and regulatory requirements
c) Financial integrity and accurate disclosure
d) Formal standards of performance and expectations
e) Harassment
f) Staffing policies
g) XXX's approach to personnel customers, competitors, suppliers, and community
h) Unacceptable ethical behavior as it applies to XXX
i) Legal obligations of XXX and its members
j) Intellectual property
k) Physical and environmental security
l) Access control
m) Proper recording or and disbursement of funds or other assets

n) Use of company and customer property
o) Internet usage
p) Drug and substance abuse policy
q) Public communication
r) Working from home,
s) Internal auditing processes
t) Political contributions
u) Preparation of resumes
v) Wage determinations and gifts and gratuities
w) Pricing policies and practices
x) Contract and invoice administration.

Copies will be available to all facilities, offices, and sub-contractors.

2.1.8 Personnel Recruitment and Selection

XXX will develop ethically responsible procedures for the recruitment and selection of personnel so as to positively influence and reinforce company culture. XXX will implement and maintain the following as applicable:

a) A policy statement precluding discrimination on grounds of ethnic origin, handicap or gender or other discrimination,
b) A signed agreement by prospective employees adhering to the Statement of Ethics Policy,
c) A documented selection procedure for employment agencies servicing XXX,
d) Criteria for evaluation of the ethics of employment agencies doing business with XXX,
e) Recording the results of the measures.

2.1.9 Contracts of Employment (as applicable)

All contracts and contracting actions will reflect the XXX Code of Ethics and Standards of Conduct.

2.2.0 Performance Review

Management will ensure that scheduled personnel performance reviews cover adherence to the policies and practices of the Corporate Responsibility Management System. Specifically:

a) XXX will describe the procedures for carrying out the above-mentioned appraisal / performance discussion, in its regulations.
b) Discussion will cover all areas and issues that can affect the work and the performance of the employee.
c) The employee to be appraised must be informed about what is required of him or her in the function that he or she is carrying out.
d) XXX will produce a standard appraisal form for use by reporting seniors in XXX, and
e) An appeals procedure.

2.2.1 Requirements for Suppliers/Subcontractors

XXX will ensure that its suppliers and subcontractors are aware of the applicable sections of our Corporate Responsibility Management System, specifically:

a) What we expect of our suppliers and subcontractors, and
b) What they have the right to expect from us.

2.2.2 Community Responsibility

XXX will develop a policy defining its responsibility to the community (i.e., district, town/city, and state/region).

2.2.3 Quality of Life

XXX will monitor its effect on the quality of life of:

a) Employees and their families,
b) The geographical area or community in which we operate and our potential to impact positively or negatively in that area or community.

2.2.4 Competition

XXX will conform to applicable statutory and regulatory requirements with regard to:

a) The development and maintenance of pricing structures,
b) Delivery terms and conditions,
c) Exclusion of supply to particular customers,
d) The use of different prices for the same level of performance.
e) Doing business with organizations that use restrictive competitive practices,
f) The fixing of prices,
g) Dividing of markets, and
h) Restrictive production or supply practices.

2.2.5 Accident Reporting

Management will develop procedures for the prompt and comprehensive reporting of safety or environmental accidents to proper authorities.

2.2.6 Emergency Preparedness and Response

XXX will develop an emergency response plan covering (as applicable):

a) Identification of potential disasters or emergencies in XXX
b) Preplanned responses
c) Emergency evacuation, aid, and assistance,
d) Safeguarding organization personnel
e) Consequence management (including drills or exercises)
f) Disaster prevention,
g) Cooperation with external aid and assistance organizations
h) Employee awareness training
i) Emergency reporting.

2.2.7 Absence Due to Illness

XXX will develop and implement procedures to investigate and reduce work related absenteeism and incapacity through illness, to include:

a) The definition of work related absenteeism and incapacity through illness.
b) Information and training for managers regarding absenteeism, and ways to address employee illness, absence, and return,
c) Maintenance of absenteeism statistics, and
d) Work related health investigation.

2.2.8 Safety and Health

XXX will develop and implement a safety and health promotion policy, to include (as applicable):

a) Occupational safety,
b) Accident prevention and safe human behavior,
c) Workplace cleanliness and sanitation (including ventilation systems),
d) Exercise and nutrition,
e) Transportation safety.

2.2.9 Working hours

XXX Inc. will develop and implement policies regarding working hours, to include:

a) Applicable statutory and regulatory requirements,
b) Core working hours,
c) Employee categories,
d) Emergency recalls,
e) Working from home,
f) Overtime, and
g) Project time and billing (if appropriate).

2.3.1 Integrity and disclosure

Management will define (as applicable) processes for:

a) Financial integrity and accurate disclosure
b) Key performance indicators and reporting of deviations
c) Management responsibilities and review
d) Safeguards (e.g., periodic inventories, reconciliations,)
e) Record keeping and retention
f) Recording and disbursement of funds
g) Risk analysis and mitigation
h) Conflicts of interests, outside interests, and related transactions
i) Timesheet and travel claim preparation, to include:
   1) Time recording
   2) Labor charging/rate determination
   3) Customer billing

j) Copyrighted or licensed materials
k) Accurate representation of data and credentials
l) Reporting adverse personnel information.

2.3.2 Personnel, Customer, and Stakeholder Satisfaction

XXX will develop a research methodology for periodic measurement of personnel, board, and stakeholders' satisfaction, to include:

a) Effectiveness of the Corporate Responsibility Management System,
b) Effectiveness of the Code of Ethics and Standards of Conduct,
c) Personnel, customer, and stakeholder feedback.

3. ASSOCIATED DOCUMENTS (Notional)

The IMS Manual
QP 56 - 01 Management Review
QP 82 – 01: Process Mapping
QP 82- 02 Internal Audits
CRM Internal Audit Checklist
QP 84 – 04 Data Analysis
Form 85-01 Corrective/Preventive Action Report and Nonconforming Product Report
International Standards ISO 9000, 14000, 28000, 31000, 22320, and BS 25999
Risk Management EXCEL Spreadsheets

APPENDIX A-1

CORPORATE RESPONSIBILITY MANAGEMENT INTERNAL AUDIT CHECKLIST

1. CORPORATE RESPONSIBILITY SYSTEM REQUIREMENTS

1.1 General

❑ Has the organization developed, documented, and implemented a Corporate Responsibility Management System (CRMS) that will:

- ○ Identify all processes and interactions
- ○ Determine the interaction between these various processes and interactions,
- ○ Determine the (ethics-based) effectiveness criteria for the implementation and monitoring of these processes,
- ○ Show the availability of resources and information relevant to the processes,
- ○ Monitor, measure, and analyze the processes
- ○ Take necessary actions to:
  - • Achieve the planned objectives,
  - • Implement corrective and preventive action, and
  - • Continuously improve the processes?

1.1 Policy and Procedural Requirements

1.2.1 General

❑ Does the CRMS include a manual, containing documented explanations of policies and objectives, and procedures required by this International Standard?

1.2.2 Corporate Responsibility Management System Manual

❑ Does the organization maintain an Corporate Responsibility Management System manual that includes:

- o The scope of the Corporate Responsibility Management System,
- o The documented procedures established for the system or reference to them, and
- o A description of the interaction between the processes of the Corporate Responsibility Management System.

2. MANAGEMENT INVOLVEMENT

2.1 Involvement of Management

❑ Does management demonstrate its social and ethical involvement with society, the governing board, other stakeholders, and own personnel by:

- o Developing, implementing, and continuously improving the Corporate Responsibility Management System,
- o Communicating to all levels in the organization the importance of satisfying the requirements, standards, and values used by the organization to carry out its business,
- o Communicating to all levels in the organization the importance of satisfying statutory and regulatory requirements in the practice of company ethics,

- Developing and implementing the company's ethics policies and objectives,
- Carrying out a program or internal audits, and
- Making resources available?

2.2 Corporate Responsibility Management Policy

❑ Has management determined a policy and ensured that the policy:

- Is suitable and contiguous with the needs of the organization,
- Is consistent with statutory and regulatory requirements,
- Provides for continuous improvement of the CRMS
- Provides the framework for development of measurable objectives,
- Is communicated to, and understood by, the whole organization,
- Is periodically assessed for its suitability?

2.3 Administration and Management

❑ Has management ensured that all responsibilities and authorities are documented and communicated through the organization, be establishing:

- The tasks, responsibilities, and authorities of all employees with respect to carrying out the formulated ethics policy.
- The tasks, responsibilities, and authorities of assigned supporting contractors, as applicable?

2.3.1 Oversight Officer

❑ Has management appointed an oversight officer, who will be responsible for the development, implementation, and maintenance of the Corporate Responsibility Management System?

- [ ] Does the Management Representative work directly for the President and periodically report on the performance of the Corporate Responsibility Management System and identify potential improvements?

2.3.2 Internal Communication

- [ ] Has management provided a structure to inform personnel about the Corporate Responsibility Management System, in which ethics management is regularly reviewed within the organization and communication takes place at all levels and functions regarding the effectiveness of the Corporate Responsibility Management System?

2.4 Management Oversight

- [ ] Does management periodically review the effectiveness of the Corporate Responsibility Management System?

- [ ] During each review, does management determine:
  - ○ If the Corporate Responsibility Management System has to be modified,
  - ○ If policies have to be modified, or objectives amended,
  - ○ The need for (or status of) corrective and corrective actions?

3 HUMAN RESOURCES

3.1 General

- [ ] Are personnel trained on the Corporate Responsibility Management System and how it applies to their positions and functions?

3.1.2 Ethics Awareness Training

❑ Has management:

- o Developed and scheduled ethics awareness training for all personnel,
- o Evaluated and measured the effectiveness of the training, and
- o Record all relevant training conducted?

3.1.2 Complaints Procedure

❑ Has management provided employees with a process for communicating instances of unacceptable behavior, to include:

- o The complaint submission procedure
- o Responsibilities for complaints procedure administration,
- o Confidentiality of complaints
- o Appeal rights of personnel accused?

3.1.4 Personnel Representation

❑ Has management created a consultative body within the organization:

- o To monitor the ethical functioning of the organization and the interests of all the employees,
- o To define objectives, tasks, responsibilities, authorities, and procedures in the operation of the Corporate Responsibility Management System,
- o To review instances of reported violations of the Corporate Responsibility Management System, and
- o To administer the organization's system of sanctions (see 6.3)?

3.2 Sanctions

❑ Has management developed a system of sanctions to include:

- ○ Definition and description undesirable ethical behavior in the organization,
- ○ The manner in which unacceptable ethical conduct is reported,
- ○ The manner in which corrective action will be taken, and
- ○ The manner in which personal information is documented and recorded?

3.3 Code of Ethics and Standards of Conduct.

❑ Has management created a *Code of Ethics and Standards of Conduct*, to include:

- ○ The Corporate Responsibility Management System,
- ○ Statutory and regulatory requirements,
- ○ Formal standards of performance and expectations,,
- ○ The organization's moral values with respect to personnel, customers, competitors, suppliers, and society,
- ○ Unacceptable ethical behavior as it applies to the organization,
- ○ Legal obligations of the organization and its members,
- ○ Intellectual property,
- ○ Physical and environmental security,
- ○ Access control,
- ○ Communications and operations management,
- ○ Use of company property,
- ○ Internet usage,
- ○ Timesheet and travel claim preparation,
- ○ Working from home,
- ○ Internal auditing processes?

4 MANAGING THE CORPORATE RESPONSIBILITY MANAGEMENT SYSTEM

4.1 Communication and Participation

❑ Does management involve all levels of the organization in the operation of the Corporate Responsibility Management System?

- ○ Do committees will ensure that meetings are recorded, and
- ○ Is sufficient time and resources are allocated?

4.2 Integrity and Disclosure

❑ Has the organization will defined (as applicable) processes for:

- ○ Financial integrity and accurate disclosure
- ○ Key performance indicators and reporting of deviations
- ○ Management responsibilities and oversight
- ○ Safeguards (e.g., periodic inventories, reconciliations,)
- ○ Record keeping and retention
- ○ Recording and disbursement of funds
- ○ Risk analysis and mitigation
- ○ Conflicts of interests, outside interests, and related transactions
- ○ Timesheet and travel claim preparation, to include:
  - ○ Time recording
  - ○ Labor charging/rate determination
  - ○ Customer billing
- ○ Copyrighted or licensed materials
- ○ Accurate representation of data and credentials
- ○ Reporting adverse personnel information.

4.3 Personnel Recruitment and Selection

❑ Has the organization developed ethically responsible procedures for the recruitment and selection of personnel so as to positively influence and reinforce company culture?

❑ Has the organization maintained the following as applicable:

- o A policy statement precluding discrimination on grounds of ethnic origin, handicap or gender or other discrimination,
- o A signed agreement by prospective employees adhering to the Statement of Ethics Policy,
- o A documented selection procedure for employment agencies servicing the organization,
- o Criteria for evaluation of the ethics of employment agencies doing business with the organization,
- o Recording the results of the measures?

4.4 Contracts of Employment

❑ Does the organization reflect the *Code of Ethics and Standards of Conduct* in its employment contracts?

4.5 Performance Review

❑ Does management ensure that scheduled personnel performance reviews cover adherence to the policies and practices of the Corporate Responsibility Management System? Specifically:

- o Does the organization describe the procedures for carrying out the above-mentioned appraisal/ performance?
- o Does discussion cover all areas and issues that can affect the work and the performance of the employee?
- o Are employees to be appraised informed about what is required of them in the function that they are carrying out?
- o Does the organization have a standard appraisal form for use by reporting seniors in the organization?
- o Is there an appeals procedure?

4.6 Requirements for Suppliers

❑ Does the organization ensure that suppliers are aware of the applicable sections of the *Code of Ethics and Standards of Conduct* and the expectations of suppliers in accordance with the *Code of Ethics and Standards of Conduct*?

4.7 Community Responsibility

❑ Is there a policy defining the organization's responsibility to the community (i.e., district, town/city, and region)?

4.8 Quality of Life

❑ Does the organization monitor its effect on the quality of life of:

   ○ Employees and their families,
   ○ Major suppliers and subcontractors
   ○ The geographical area in which it operates and has potential to impact positively or negatively?

4.9 Competition

❑ Does the organization conform to applicable statutory and regulatory requirements with regard to:

   ○ The development and maintenance of pricing structures
   ○ Delivery terms and conditions
   ○ Exclusion of supply to particular customers
   ○ The use of different prices for the same level of performance
   ○ Doing business with organizations that use restrictive competitive practices
   ○ The fixing of prices or dividing of markets
   ○ Restrictive production or supply practices?

4.10 Accident Reporting

❑ Has the organization developed procedures for directly reporting safety or environmental accidents to proper authority?

4.11 Hazardous Materials

❑ Has the organization will developed (as applicable) procedures to prevent or reduce the environmental risks related to the storage, transfer and transport of dangerous materials? Specifically:

  ○ Adherence to National laws and regulations, guidelines, decisions, and permits,
  ○ Responsibilities for carrying out formulated policy,
  ○ Procedures for the storage, transfer and transport of dangerous materials,
  ○ Training and qualifications of users?

4.12 Pollution Prevention

❑ Has the organization developed (as applicable) pollution prevention procedures to include:

  ○ Identification of all potential sources of pollution, wastes, and emissions,
  ○ Identification of all applicable statutory and regulatory requirements.
  ○ Reduction measures
  ○ Recycling opportunities?

❑ Does the organization discuss the operation of the pollution prevention procedures at scheduled Management Reviews and record discussions, nonconformities, and corrective and preventive actions?

4.13 Energy Conservation

❏ Has the organization developed an Energy Conservation Program, to include:

- An energy conservation policy,
- Recognition of all applicable environmental laws and regulations and the conditions that are stipulated in the environmental license as applicable),
- A survey identifying all sources of energy expenditure and the technical and economic feasibility of implementing specific energy conservation measures.
- Periodic evaluation of the system during the internal audits and management reviews?

4.14 Environmental Assessment

❏ Does the organization carry out, or have carried out a survey into the environmental aspects of the activities, and into alternatives for those activities which constitute a potential burden on the environment?

4.14.1 Environmental Aspects

❏ Has the organization identified all relevant environmental aspects of products and services, to include:

- A purchasing policy reflecting for products and services with potential environmental impact,
- Criteria and selection of the most suitable suppliers?

4.15 Competence, Experience, and Training

❏ Has the organization established requirements with regard to the education and instruction of all personnel and set standards for competence, experience, and training in the following areas related to the Corporate Responsibility Management System. Specifically:

- o Occupational Safety and Health,
- o Energy conservation
- o Hazardous Material Control and Management
- o Pollution prevention, and
- o Recycling.
- o Contracting,
- o Procurement,
- o Internal auditing, and
- o Finance and accounting?

4.16 Risk Assessment and Minimization

❑ Has the organization implemented risk assessment and minimization procedures for all activities and components, in order to:

- o Determine a relative ranking of potential risks, and determine the likely frequencies and consequences of those risks,
- o Recognize opportunities as well as risks, and
- o Formalize and document knowledge for more precise decision-making?

4.17 Emergency Preparedness and Response

❑ Has the organization developed an emergency response plan covering:

- o Identification of potential disasters or emergencies in the organization
- o Preplanned responses
- o Emergency evacuation, aid, and assistance,
- o Safeguarding organization personnel
- o Consequence management (including drills or exercises)
- o Disaster prevention,
- o Cooperation with external aid and assistance organizations
- o Employee awareness training

- o Emergency reporting?

4.18 Absence Due to Illness

❑ Does the organization have documented procedures with regard to work related absenteeism and incapacity through illness, to include:

- o The definition of work related absenteeism and incapacity through illness.
- o Social and medical counseling of employees who are ill or incapacitated. or who are returning to the workplace,
- o Information and training for managers regarding absenteeism, and ways to address employee illness, absence, and return,
- o Maintenance of absenteeism statistics, and
- o Work related health investigation?

4.19 Safety and Health

❑ Does the organization have a published safety and health promotion policy, to include:

- o Occupational safety,
- o Accident prevention and safe human behavior,
- o Workplace cleanliness and sanitation (including ventilation systems),
- o Exercise and nutrition,
- o Transportation safety?

4.20 Working hours

❑ Does the organization have written policies regarding working hours, to include:

- o Applicable statutory and regulatory requirements,
- o Core working hours,
- o Employee categories,
- o Emergency recalls,

- o Working from home,
- o Overtime, and
- o Charge number usage (if appropriate)?

5. METRICS ESTABLISHMENT

5.1 General

❏ Does the organization have documented procedures to monitor and measure, the key characteristics of its operations and activities that can have significant impact on the professional and business ethics of the organization?

5.1.1 Personnel, Customer, and Stakeholder Satisfaction

❏ Does the organization have a research methodology for periodic measurement of personnel, board, and stakeholders' satisfaction, to include:

- o Effectiveness of the Corporate Responsibility Management System,
- o Effectiveness of the Code of Ethics and Standards of Conduct,
- o Personnel, customer, and stakeholder feedback?

5.1.2 Internal Reviews

❏ Does the organization will conduct periodic internal reviews to determine the effectiveness of the Corporate Responsibility Management System, in order to:

- o Determine whether or not the Corporate Responsibility Management System conforms to the organization's requirements and to statutory and regulatory requirements

❏ Has the internal audit system been properly implemented and maintained?

❏ Are the results of reviews provided to management?

5.2 Nonconformance and Corrective and Preventive Action

❏ Does the organization have procedures for defining responsibility and authority for ethical nonconformities, taking action to mitigate any impacts caused and for initiating and completing corrective and preventive action?

❏ Are corrective or preventive actions taken to eliminate the cause of actual or potential nonconformities appropriate for the magnitude of the problem and commensurate with actual or potential impact?

5.3 Continual Improvement

❏ Does the organization continually improve the effectiveness of the Corporate Responsibility Management System by using policy, objectives, audit results, data analysis, research into personnel, customer, and stakeholders' satisfaction, corrective and preventive measures and management review meetings?

❏ When shortcomings are detected from audit results, data analyses, satisfaction surveys, or management reviews, does the organization ensure that timely corrective and preventive measures are taken?

❏ Is the effectiveness of measures taken documented?

APPENDIX THREE

A ROBUST, REPLICABLE, AND DEFENSIBLE RISK MANAGEMENT STRATEGY

> **CEO Note:** *I refer to risk management as "disciplined subjectivity" because you subjectively assess your threats, criticalities, and vulnerabilities by using your knowledge and experience. But, you assign them a consistent, replicable set of numerical values or "criteria". You cannot do risk management just by assessing risks in your head, or by yourself. I have developed risk management processes like the process identified below for both Military and civilian applications. Try it and contact me if you have any questions. You'll like it.*

The terms *risk analysis*, *risk assessment*, and *risk management*, often used interchangeably, can mean a variety of different concepts and/or metrics. In point of fact, there is no one single approach to risk management. Approaches and strategies can be as simple or complex.

A properly conducted security risk assessment allows decisions to be made based on realistic scenario assumptions and provides justification for commitment of program resources.

the processes they were made to assess. However, simpler is almost always better, and using a spreadsheet that automatically computes and displays the assessments is better still.

Doing risk management on a spreadsheet customized for your organization can provide you with a fast, descriptive tool to:

- Standardize, assess, prioritize, and display readiness for specific business or mission scenarios
- Predict the impact of personnel and material changes before time or funds are expended
- Create uniform reports to higher authority
- Predict readiness by assessing risks.

Functions (e.g., sums, multiplications, averages) can be programmed into the spreadsheet, and graphs can be created automatically as values are introduced or changed, as will be shown.

This chapter develops a risk management program for your organization that:

- Identifies the threats (i.e., hazards or adverse events) to the organization
- Predicts the probability of the threat occurring
- Predicts the consequences of the threat occurring.[35]

Then, (and unlike more basic risk prediction models):

- Predicts the impact of one or more external or environmental factors; and finally
- Predicts the change if a selected course of action (COA) is implemented.[36]

---

[35] We refer to this as computing basic risk assessment.

[36] This is advanced risk assessment, leading the way to meaningful risk *management.*

Creating risk assessment criteria

For assessments to be consistent, and reports to be uniform among reporting departments, and for the management tool we are creating to help in the decision making process, we need standard numerical values or "criteria" to assess:

- Threats to the mission or operation
- Vulnerability of the mission or process to threats
- Criticality of the process to the overall mission of the organization.

A basic EXCEL spreadsheet model, consisting of a set of connected worksheets, can be a priceless management tool for the CEO, because it forces him/her to:

- Identify the major potential threats to the mission of the organization
- Prioritize them, by assigning a numerical value to each (to be explained later)
- Evaluate the criticality of the part of the mission potentially impacted by the threat in terms of a numerical value
- Evaluate the vulnerability of the mission or organization to impact by the threat in terms of a numerical value.

Table 1 contains a notional set of numerical values from 1 to 10 and defines each in terms of threat, criticality, and vulnerability. These are the numbers we will use to complete the risk assessment process.

Table 1 The Criteria Table

Level	Scale	Threat Criteria	Criticality Criteria	Vulnerability Criteria
Lowest	1,2	Never occurred before - unlikely; minimally effective due to physical area/ environment; not a significant source of disruption	Minimally disruptive to mission if used	Minimally vulnerable to attack, due to own tactics, equipment, physical surroundings
Low	3,4	Has occurred before - possible; effective in physical area for short period; potential source of disruption	Disruptive to mission if used; minor mission degradation	Susceptible to attack, but history and physical surroundings make attack unlikely
Medium	5,6	Occurs periodically and predictably; likely to encounter; disruptive when occurring	Mission degraded, but can continue if attacked; some casualties	Highly vulnerable to attack, due to own tactical limitations and physical surroundings
High	7,8	Occurs often; enemy has expertise; utility in area against missions, expect to encounter; highly disruptive	Mission seriously degraded, but can continue marginally if attacked; significant casualties possible	Extremely vulnerable due to tactical and equipment limitations and physical surroundings
Highest	9,10	High probability of use; enemy proficient in use; unlimited utility and effectiveness against most missions; catastrophic if used	Mission failure; much disruption likely	Imminent danger, due to nature of operations, plus equipment limitations

The Threat Assessment Spreadsheet

Table 2 is an example of a threat assessment matrix or threat assessment spreadsheet. The notional missions or processes of the organization are listed on the vertical axis and the potential threats along the horizontal axis. Once you have identified both, it remains only to assign subjective numerical values from the Criteria Table.

Our spreadsheets contain normally expected organizational processes and eight notional threats to those processes. Risk managers, having identified the threats, assign numbers from the Criteria Table, based on their knowledge and experience. The spreadsheet automatically computes the total and the average threat[37]. We use the average threat in all the subsequent calculations.

Some users use the highest threat figure in the row instead of the average threat figure. That's OK, as long as they use it consistently throughout the risk assessment process. The user may want to modify any or all of these matrices and calculations to suit his/her own preferences. Some modifications may prove misleading or self-defeating (such as using "0"). You will find them out soon enough. It is only important to be *consistent* throughout your process.

---

[37] This is the simplest way I have found to do this. You may have another way. You must, however, be consistent in whatever method you develop.

Table 2 Sample threat assessment matrix

Organizational Tasks	Terrorist Attack	Utility Loss	Hacker/Cyber Attack	Industrial Espionage	Strike	Agent Spill	Natural Disaster	Falsified reporting	Total	Average
Product Design	9	4	9	9	3	5	8	8	55	7
Product Development	4	4	9	9	3	5	8	8	50	6
Manufacturing	9	9	9	5	3	5	8	8	56	7
Measurement & Testing	9	4	9	5	6	5	8	8	54	7
Internal Movement	9	4	6	5	6	5	8	8	51	6
Warehousing	6	4	8	5	3	5	8	8	46	6
Marketing	4	4	6	5	3	5	8	8	43	5
Accounting	4	4	7	5	3	5	8	8	44	6
Planning	4	4	8	5	3	5	8	8	45	6
Shipping	9	4	6	5	6	5	8	8	51	6
Receiving	5	4	6	5	6	5	8	8	47	6
Misc. Clerical	4	4	7	5	3	5	8	8	44	6
Order Processing	6	4	4	7	6	5	8	8	48	6
Customer Sales & Service	4	4	6	5	6	5	8	8	46	6
Document Retrieval	8	4	6	5	3	5	8	8	47	6
Command & Control	4	4	6	8	3	5	8	8	46	6
Data Analysis	7	4	6	8	3	5	8	8	49	6
General Management	7	4	6	5	6	5	8	8	49	6

The model uses the "Average" threat values, which automatically post to the risk assessment spreadsheet.[38]

Computing Unadjusted Risk

As the planners complete the threat spreadsheet they identify and assess the threats to the organization. The next spreadsheet automatically copies the computed average threat for each organizational task and allows us to compute unadjusted (i.e., basic) risk according to the formula:

Risk = Criticality x Vulnerability x Threat

To determine unadjusted risk, the planner now assigns numerical values from the (same) Criteria Table for:

- The *criticality* of the threat incident or adverse event (if it happened) to the specific organizational task; and
- The *vulnerability* of the organization to the threat incident or adverse event.

How *vulnerable* the organization may be is a function of what actions it either must take or has already taken to mitigate

---

[38] The shaded columns are posted or computed automatically by the software.

or preclude the threat or event. For example, posting extra security personnel or adding alarm systems decreases an organization's *vulnerability* to a break-in. The alarm systems have not decreased the threat of a break-in, or the criticality of a break-in; only the vulnerability. Accordingly, <u>you reduce risk by reducing vulnerability.</u> Realizing this is essential for the CEO and risk manager. Table 3 computes basic risk assessment. This is often the final step in risk *assessment,* but it is only the beginning of risk *management,* as you will see in the pages that follow. [39]

Table 3 Computing basic risk

Organizational Tasks	Criticality	Vulnerability	Threat	Risk
Product Design	8	6	7	330
Product Development	8	5	6	250
Manufacturing	8	5	7	280
Measurement & Testing	8	4	7	216
Internal Movement	5	5	6	159
Warehousing	7	6	6	236
Marketing	4	7	5	151
Accounting	5	6	6	165
Planning	8	5	6	225
Shipping	5	4	6	128
Receiving	4	7	6	165
Misc. Clerical	4	5	6	110
Order Processing	4	5	6	120
Customer Sales & Service	7	6	6	242
Document Retrieval	8	6	6	282
Command & Control	4	6	6	138
Data Analysis	5	6	6	184
General Management	5	6	6	184

---

[39] The shaded columns are posted or computed automatically, and the numbers are rounded off. You don't have to do anything with them.

Advanced risk assessment calculation #1: Assessing the impact of the external environment

Risk = Criticality x Vulnerability x Threat x Environmental Adjustment

I originally added this step to the modeling process to assess the impact of host nation support on military logistic operations overseas. In some cases, host nation support/ involvement was invaluable, as with assignment of interpreters or counterparts. In other cases, (e.g., corrupt bureaucracies), U.S. forces were often better left alone. Organizations wanting to separately reflect this often critical variable can add this step to assess:

- Foreign country support (receipt, transportation, customs, etc.)
- Supply chain security
- Outsourcing (foreign or domestic)
- Special laws, regulations, or protocols
- Anything else you want to separate from the internal processes but you feel must be included in the overall risk assessment process.

To show the impact of the external factors (whatever you decide to call them), multiply the computed basic risk by the number determined from table 3-4.

Table 4 Representative external environment numerical values and narrative descriptions

Scale	Criteria
0.1 - 0.5	Invaluable support - enhanced mission conduct and efficiency 0.6 - 0.9 Effective - minimal mission support
0.6-0.9	Effective - minimal mission support
1.0	No significant support or degradation
1.1 – 1.4	Degradation of mission, making accomplishment difficult to very difficult, with increasingly greater mission vulnerability; mission less safe/less efficient
1.5 – 2.0	Severe degradation with possible to likely mission failure

For example, if the addition of a certain procedure or custom in the country where your process is outsourced decreases the risk by half, you multiply the risk figure by .5. If the practice makes no appreciable difference, multiply the risk by 1 (no change). If a procedure makes it half again as difficult or risky, multiply by 1.5. Again, this will not corrupt or hinder your computations, as long as you apply it consistently.

Table 5 shows the addition of the column marked "Environmental Adjustment".

Table 5 Computing the Environmental Adjustment

Organizational Tasks	Criticality	Vulnerability	Threat	Risk	Environment Adjustment	Adj Risk(1)
Product Design	8	6	7	330	0.9	297
Product Development	8	5	6	250	0.2	50
Manufacturing	8	5	7	280	0.4	112
Measurement & Testing	8	4	7	216	0.5	108
Internal Movement	5	5	6	159	0.3	48
Warehousing	7	6	6	236	0.7	165
Marketing	4	7	5	151	0.9	135
Accounting	5	6	6	165	0.8	132
Planning	8	5	6	225	0.3	68
Shipping	5	4	6	128	0.3	38
Receiving	4	7	6	165	0.5	82
Misc. Clerical	4	5	6	110	0.6	66
Order Processing	4	5	6	120	0.7	84
Customer Sales & Service	7	6	6	242	0.5	121
Document Retrieval	8	6	6	282	1.1	310
Command & Control	4	6	6	138	0.3	41
Data Analysis	5	6	6	184	0.3	55
General Management	5	6	6	184	0.3	55

Graphing unadjusted and adjusted risk

Now, you can quantify the impact of the environmental factors and get a more accurate assessment of the risk involved, displaying the impact graphically as shown in figure 1. Note the bars for "Shipping", where environmental factors (e.g., adverse flying conditions) make the risk greater.

Figure 1 Unadjusted and adjusted risk

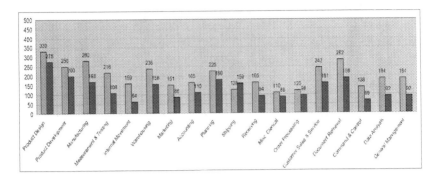

Advanced risk assessment #2: Identifying and assessing potential courses of action – now comes the fun

Identifying threats, criticalities, and vulnerabilities in accordance with a standard set of numerical values to provide a "snapshot" of operations is normally the extent of the basic risk assessment process. However, risk *assessment* becomes risk *management* when the CEO goes beyond what he has just completed, to identify and evaluate potential courses of action (COAs) before any time or funding is expended (or wasted). [40]

Implementing a new course of action to an existing mission, operation, or project does not change the *threat* to the mission. Neither does it change the *criticality* of the mission. It does (or should), however, change the *vulnerability* of the mission in the organization.

We now employ the following formula to show the impact of the course of action on the risk:

Risk = Threat x Criticality x Revised Vulnerability x Environmental Adjustment

---

[40] ISO 9001 2015 uses the term "opportunities".

Identifying potential COAs and modeling them in the risk assessment can be expected to show:

- Significant reductions of risk in one or more capability areas if implemented (good)
- Small or insignificant risk reductions if implemented (neither good nor bad)
- A potential increase in risk in another part of the mission if implemented (bad).

Table 6 takes the basic risk computation we did earlier but goes on to reflect the impact of the external environment (for better or worse) and the impact of the revised vulnerability. You now have a real snapshot of the present and your best possible prediction (albeit subjective) of the future – if you implement a particular course of action (or series of courses of action). [41]

Table 6 Computing risk after COA implementation

Organizational Tasks	Criticality	Vulnerability	Threat	Risk	Environment	Adj Risk(1)		Adj Risk(2)
					Adjustment		Revised Vulnerability	(COA)
Product Design	8	8	7	330	0.9	297	5	248
Product Development	8	5	6	250	0.2	50	4	40
Manufacturing	8	5	7	280	0.4	112	3	67
Measurement & Testing	8	4	7	216	0.5	108	2	54
Internal Movement	5	5	6	150	0.3	48	2	19
Warehousing	7	6	6	238	0.7	165	4	110
Marketing	4	7	5	151	0.9	135	4	77
Accounting	5	6	6	165	0.8	132	4	88
Planning	8	5	6	225	0.3	68	4	54
Shipping	5	4	6	128	0.3	38	5	48
Receiving	4	7	6	165	0.5	82	4	47
Misc. Clerical	4	5	6	110	0.6	66	4	53
Order Processing	4	5	6	120	0.7	84	4	67
Customer Sales & Service	7	6	6	242	0.5	121	4	81
Document Retrieval	8	6	6	282	1.1	310	4	207
Command & Control	4	6	6	138	0.3	41	3	21
Data Analysis	5	6	6	184	0.3	55	3	28
General Management	5	6	6	184	0.3	55	3	28

---

[41] Again, the shaded columns are computed automatically.

171

Risk assessment at a glance – telling the story

If you work with spreadsheets, you already know how to create and revise graphs automatically. [42] Figure 2, the automatically developed graph shows:

- The unadjusted (basic) risk assessment
- The impact (for better or worse) of the external environment on the assessed risk
- The impact of a notional course of action, which is the result of revising the numerical value for *vulnerability*.

Figure 2 The Total Risk Management Picture

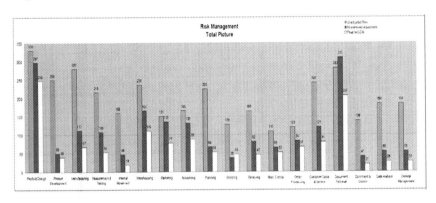

Again, our figures are notional in order to show the utility of the model and to suggest that all relevant factors need to be considered. They are not from any specific project.

It is not unusual to discover that simulating the implementation of potential courses of action (i.e., "gaming" them) predicts only small or insignificant changes. That's OK! In fact, modeling can show the CEO that certain courses of action may not be worth the time or expense. You need to know that before you waste time and money. It is also a good way to impress your bosses or the Board.

---

[42] Once constructed, the graph changes automatically when the values in the table change.

The Rest of the Story – Describing Urgency

Having done all the work, it remains to tell the rest of the story by defining "urgency". That is, which are the highest risks and, therefore, the most urgent to correct or mitigate. We will do that with a simple stoplight chart, developed as follows:

1. The highest number we developed in the risk assessment process was 330.
2. We want to create three categories of urgency: Critical, Necessary, and Routine, shown in red, yellow, and green respectively.
3. Accordingly, we divide 1- 330 in three equal parts (1-110, 111-220, and 221-330). Table 7 describes the categories of urgency.

Table 7 Creating Categories of Urgency

Organizational Tasks	Urgency
221-330	Critical
111-220	Necessary
1-110	Routine

Table 8 is the final table and stoplight chart as shown below.

Table 8 Risk Urgency Chart

Organizational Tasks	Risk	Env. Adj	COA	Adj. Risk	After COA
Product Design	330	297	248	Critical	Critical
Product Development	250	50	40	Routine	Routine
Manufacturing	280	112	67	Necessary	Routine
Measurement & Testing	216	108	54	Routine	Routine
Internal Movement	159	48	19	Routine	Routine
Warehousing	236	165	110	Necessary	Routine

Marketing	151	135	**77**	Necessary	Routine
Accounting	165	132	**88**	Necessary	Routine
Planning	225	68	**54**	Routine	Routine
Shipping	128	38	**48**	Routine	Routine
Receiving	165	82	**47**	Routine	Routine
Misc. Clerical	110	66	**53**	Routine	Routine
Order Processing	120	84	**67**	Routine	Routine
Customer Sales & Service	242	121	**81**	Necessary	Routine
Document Retrieval	282	310	**207**	Critical	Necessary
Command & Control	138	41	**21**	Routine	Routine
Data Analysis	184	55	**28**	Routine	Routine
General Management	184	55	**28**	Routine	Routine

Note the following:

- We automatically apply the environmental adjustments to the "Urgency".
- The risk mitigations developed for "Product Design" are insufficient. Either greater mitigation will be needed or the effort and expense involved will be assigned to something else.
- Risk mitigation in the area of "Document Retrieval" can reduce the urgency of the risk from urgent to necessary.
- Mitigation is expected to change the urgency of five tasks from Necessary to Routine.

Many tasks are already within our definition of routine urgency (as shown in green). According to our criteria, further correction or mitigation can be achieved with only routine effort.

Potential Benefits of a Structured Risk Management Process

Here is a summary of the potential benefits of conducting structured risk assessments in your organization.

1. Risks are identified, as well as their effects and interactions.
2. Contingency plans/courses of action can be developed, including preemptive responses which mitigate or reduce the potential impacts.
3. Expected costs can reduced, and an appropriate balance between costs and risk exposure achieved, usually with a reduced risk exposure.
4. Feedback into the design phases and planning stages is developed as part of the evaluation of risk vs. expected cost balance.
5. Opportunities and responses are recognized and gamed in advance.
6. The integration of planning and cost control is improved.
7. Members of the project team develop an analytical understanding of the likely problems and responses in their own areas, and problems in other areas which will impact on them.
8. Specific problem areas are highlighted for further analysis.
9. Management is provided with a means of signaling trends without redefining objectives.
10. Knowledge and judgments are formalized and documented, making projects easier to manage throughout their life cycles.
11. External technical, environmental, and political influences are specifically measured in direct relation to internal issues, and appropriate strategies are developed reflecting both.
12. Probability distributions are can be developed for estimating costs and completion dates.

Summary

An effective Security Risk Management strategy should include identifying (as appropriate):

- Physical failure threats and risks, such as functional failure, incidental damage, malicious damage, or terrorist or criminal action
- Operational threats and risks, including the control of security, human factors, and other activities that affect the organization's performance, condition, or safety
- Environmental or cultural aspects which may either enhance or impair security measures and equipment
- Factors outside of the organization's control such as failures in externally supplied (e.g., outsourced) equipment and services
- Stakeholder threats and risks, such as failure to meet regulatory requirements
- Security equipment, including replacement, maintenance, information and data management, and communications
- Any other threats to the continuity of operations.

Security Risk Management is the foundation of an organization's emergency management program. A properly conducted security risk assessment allows decisions to be made based on realistic scenario assumptions and provides justification for commitment of program resources.

Regardless of where the assessment leads, you will have completed a rigorous and structured (albeit subjective) assessment process, and arrived at logical, defensible, conclusions.

APPENDIX FOUR

GLOSSARY

Integrated Management Systems routinely use the following terms and definitions.

Accountability

"Having to report to, explain, justify; being responsible, answerable". (Note: Early management textbooks and courses routinely linked authority with responsibility, stating that one cannot exist without the other. Unfortunately, accountability was not always included.)

Asset

Anything that has value to the organization

Audit

A systematic, independent, and documented process for obtaining quantifiable evidence, and evaluating it objectively to determine the extent to which the Integrated Management System (IMS) audit criteria are being fulfilled. The audit can be internal (i.e., by qualified personnel) or external (i.e., by qualified personnel from outside the organization).

Auditor

Qualified, unbiased person (inside or outside the organization) with the competence to conduct an effective, meaningful, audit and produce quantifiable results

Availability

The property of being accessible and usable upon demand by an authorized entity

Confidentiality

The property that information is not made available or disclosed to unauthorized individuals, entities, or processes

Continual Improvement

Recurring mindset and processes for enhancing the Integrated Management System, leading to a better and more effective organization. This includes improvements in overall performance consistent with the organization's quality, environmental, and security management policies.

Contaminant

A foreign or unwanted material that enters and harms the environment in a measurable way

Corrective action

An action taken to ensure a proven nonconformity does not re-occur

Cost

The amount of resources needed to achieve a particular objective

Cost analysis

Estimate of the resources that to be expended to achieve a particular objective

Cost/benefit analysis

A method of providing top management with quantitative data for informed decision making

Cost avoidance

The result, expressed in dollars and cents; of changing an operation to make it more efficient

Customer

An organization or person that receives a product and may include clients, purchasers, partners, stakeholders, or any other party having a quality related relationship with you and your Organization.

Document

Information and its supporting medium; documents can be paper, magnetic, electronic, or optical computer disc, photograph or master sample, or a combination thereof.

Downstream

Refers to the actions, processes and movements (e.g., of cargo in the supply chain) that occur after the product leaves the direct operational control of the organization, including but not limited to insurance, finance, data management, and the packing, storing and transferring of cargo

Due Diligence

Investigation by or on behalf of an intended buyer of a business to check that it has the desired assets, turnover, profits, market share positions, technology, customer franchise, patents and brand rights, contracts and other attributes required by the buyer or claimed by the seller

Energy Conservation

The optimum use of all leadership and management skills, plus all available technologies to protect the environment, reduce operating costs, and enhance competitiveness

Environment

Surroundings in which an organization operates, including air, water, land, natural resources, terrain, flora, fauna, humans, surrounding communities, and their interrelations. Surroundings in this context extend from within an organization to the global system.

Environmental aspect

An element of an organization's activities or products or services with the potential to impact the environment. A significant environmental aspect has or can have significant environmental impact (e.g., the creation of hazardous waste as a byproduct).

Environmental impact

Any change to the environment whether adverse or beneficial, wholly or partially resulting from an organization's environmental aspects.

Environmental objective

An end condition that an organization strives to achieve, consistent with its environmental policy

Environmental performance

Measurable results of the organization's management of its environmental aspects

Feedback

Communication (in whatever form) that you receive regarding some action that your organization is planning to take, or has already taken. It is an indispensable part of the decision-making process, whether in strategic planning or in day-to-day operations. Ideally, it is *continuous information on performance against standards.*

Follow-up

Checking on the success or failure of a process implemented, a process changed, an order given, or some other modification done with thought to making something better or, in some way, adding value. For instance, a process modification developed to solve a quality issue on the factory floor, could result in one of the following:

Information Security

Preservation of confidentiality, integrity, and availability of information; in addition, other properties such as authenticity, accountability, non-repudiation and reliability can also be involved

Information Security Event

An identified occurrence of a system, service or network state indicating a possible breach of information security policy or failure of safeguards, or a previously unknown situation that may be security relevant

Information Security Incident

A single or a series of unwanted or unexpected information security events that have a significant probability of compromising business operations and threatening information security

Information Security Management System (ISMS)

That part of the overall management system, based on a business risk approach, to establish, implement, operate, monitor, review, maintain and improve information security. The management system includes organizational structure, policies, planning activities, responsibilities, practices, procedures, processes and resources.

Integrated Management System (IMS)

Set of interrelated management systems, functions, and disciplines used to establish policy and objectives and ways to achieve and continually improve those objectives. A typical IMS can include ISO 9000, ISO 14000, ISO 27000, ISO 28000 and MVO 8000 as described in this book.

Integrity

The property of safeguarding the accuracy and completeness of assets

Interested Party

Person or group concerned with or affected by the environmental performance of an organization.

Internal Audit/Review

Systematic, independent and documented process for obtaining audit evidence and evaluating it objectively to determine the extent to which the management system audit criteria set by the organization are fulfilled

KPI's

Key Performance Indicators are measurable, replicable, and "audit-able" metrics that Management can use to continuously assess its performance

Nonconformity

Non-fulfilment of a requirement

Organization

Company, corporation, firm, enterprise, authority or institution, or part or combination thereof, whether incorporated or not, public or private, that has its own functions and administration.

Preventive action

An action taken before an error actually occurs so as to prevent a failure from occurring.

Pollutant

A chemical, particulate, or refuse material that impairs the purity of water, air, or soil

Pollution

The destruction or impairment of a natural environment's purity by contaminants

Pollution Prevention

Use of processes, practices, techniques, materials, products, services or energy to avoid, reduce or control (separately or in combination) the creation, emission or discharge of any type of pollutant or waste, in order to reduce adverse environmental impacts. Pollution prevention can include source reduction or elimination, process, product or service changes, efficient use of resources, material and energy substitution reuse, recovery, recycling, reclamation and treatment.

Procedure

Documented and specified method or practice, in which to carry out an activity or a process

Product

The "result of a process" and may include any services or advice, provided to a client as well as physical goods.

Process

A set of interrelated or interacting activities that transforms inputs into outputs. In simple terms, what you do to create or accomplish something.

Record

A "document stating the results achieved or providing evidence of activities performed". It may be retained electronically or on paper

Residual risk

The risk remaining after risk treatment

Risk

The chance of injury, damage, or loss; risks cannot be avoided entirely, but can be identified and (to varying degrees) reduced or mitigated.

Risk acceptance

A decision to accept a risk

Risk analysis

Systematic use of information to identify risk, assign consistent numerical values, and to predict the impact of the risk on the mission and operations of

Risk assessment

The overall process of risk analysis and risk evaluation

Risk evaluation process of comparing the estimated risk against given risk criteria to determine the significance of the risk

Risk management means the coordinated activities to track, prioritize, mitigate, or eliminate risk to the missions and operations

Risk treatment

The process of selection and implementation of measures to modify risk

Service Realization

Delivery of services that meet all customer, and regulatory requirements

Security

Resistance to intentional, unauthorized act(s) designed to cause harm or damage to, or by, the supply chain

Security management

Systematic and coordinated activities and practices through which an organization optimally manages its risks and the associated potential threats and impacts therefrom

Security management objective

Specific outcome or achievement required of security in order to meet the security management policy. It is essential that such outcomes are linked either directly or indirectly to providing the products, supply or services delivered by the total business to its customers or end users.

Security management policy

Overall intentions and direction of an organization, related to the security and the framework for the control of security-related processes and activities that are derived from and consistent with the organization's policy and regulatory requirements

Security management programs

Means by which a security management objective is achieved

Security management target

Specific level of performance required to achieve a security management objective

Stakeholder

Person or entity having a vested interest in the organization's performance, success or the impact of its activities; examples include customers, shareholders, financiers, insurers, regulators, statutory bodies, employees, contractors, suppliers, labor organizations, or society.

Supplier

An "organization or person that provides a product". A supplier can be internal or external to the Organization. In a contractual situation a supplier may be referred to as a contractor.

References

1. Juran, J.M. *Juran on Planning for Quality*, The Free Press, New York, NY, 1988

2. Svara, J. *The Ethics Primer for Public Administrators in Government and Nonprofit Organizations*, Jones and Bartlett Publishers, Sudbury, MA, 2007

3. H. Mitzberg, *The Rise and Fall of Strategic Planning*, The Free Press,, New York, NY, 1994

4. R.S. Kaplan, D.P. Norton, *Strategy Maps, Converting Intangible Assets into Tangible Outcomes*, Boston, MA Harvard University Press, 2004

5. Defense Acquisition University, *Introduction to Defense Acquisition Management*, DAU Press, Fort Belvoir, VA 2005

6. L.R. Bittel, Ed, *Encyclopedia of Professional Management*. New York: McGraw-Hill Book Co., 1978

7. J. Ansel and F. Wharton, *Risk, Analysis, Assessment and Management*. New York, NY: J. Wiley & Sons, 1992

8. S. Crainer, Ed, *The Financial Times Handbook of Management – the state of the art*, Pitman Publishing, London, 1995

9. M.L. Marks and P.H. Mirvis, *Joining Forces, Making One Plus One Equal Three in Mergers, Acquisitions, and Alliances.* Institute for Management Studies, Reno, NV, San Francisco: Josey-Bass Publishers, 1998

10. W.R. Shilling, ed. *Nontraditional Warfare, Twenty-First Century Threats and Responses,* Dulles, VA: Brassey's Inc., 2002

11. D.S. Alberts et al., *Network Centric Warfare, Developing and Leveraging Information Superiority,* CCRP Publications Series, 1999

12. W. Schwartau, ed. *Information Warfare,* 2nd ed. New York: Thunder's Mouth Press, 1994

13. Kerzner, H. *Project Management, A Systems Approach to Planning, Scheduling, and Controlling,* 2nd Ed, Van Nostrand Reinhold Co., NY, 1984

14. Dluhy, M.J. and Chen, K (Ed), *Interdisciplinary Planning: A Perspective for the Future,* Center for Urban Policy Research, New Brunswick, NJ 1986

15. Bennett, S.J., et. al, *Corporate Realities & Environmental Truths Strategies For Leading Your Business in The Environmental Era,* John Wiley & Sons, New York NY, 1993

16. Callenback, E. et al, *EcoManagement, The Elmwood Guide to Ecological Auditing and Sustainable Business,* Berrett-Koehler Publishers, San Francisco, CA, 1993

17. Hirschhorn, J.S., *Prosperity Without Pollution – The Prevention Strategy for Industry and Consumers,* Van Nostrand Reinhold, New York, NY 1991

18. R. C. Nash, J. Cibinic, *Competitive Negotiation: The Source Selection Process,* George Washington University, Press, Washington DC, 1993

19. A. Kossiakoff, W.N. Sweet, *Systems Engineering Principles and Practice*, J. Wiley & Sons, Hoboken, NJ, 2003

20. B. S. Blanchard, *System Engineering Management*, 3rd Edition, J. Wiley & Sons, Hoboken, NJ, 2004

21. N.S. Foy, *Computer Management - A Common Sense Approach*, Auerback Publishers, Philadelphia, PA, 1972

22. R.K. Elliott, J.J. Willingham, *Management Fraud, Detection and Deterrence*, Petrocelli Books, Inc., New York, NY, 1980

Other Books by Eugene A. Razzetti

Other books by Gene Razzetti:

1. *The Executive's Guide to Corporate Responsibility Management and MVO 8000 (2nd Ed)*

2. *Fixes That Last – The Executive's Guide to Fix It or Lose It Management (2nd Ed)*

3. *The Executive's Guide To Internal Auditing*

4. *Hardening by Auditing*

All books are available hard copy or electronically through all the usual channels.

About the Author

Eugene A. (Gene) Razzetti retired from the U.S. Navy as a Captain in 1992, a Vietnam Veteran and having had two at-sea and two major shore commands. Since then, he has been an independent management consultant, project manager, and ISO auditor. He became an adjunct military analyst with the Center for Naval Analyses after September 11, 2001. He has authored four management books, articles for professional journals, and co-authored MVO 8000, a Corporate Responsibility Management Standard. He has served on boards and committees dealing with ethics and professionalism in the practice of management consulting. He is a senior member of the American Society for Quality (ASQ) and assisted the Government of Guatemala with markedly heightening the environmental and security postures of its two principal commercial port facilities.

He can be reached at www.corprespmgmt.com or generazz@ aol.com.

Printed in the United States
By Bookmasters